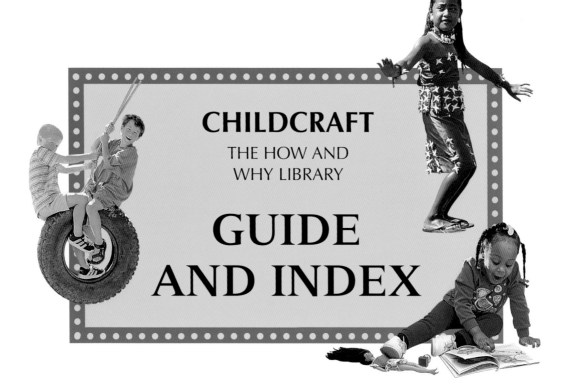

CHILDCRAFT
THE HOW AND WHY LIBRARY

GUIDE
AND INDEX

World Book, Inc.
a Scott Fetzer company
Chicago

Childcraft—The How and Why Library

© 2007 World Book, Inc. All rights reserved. This volume may not be reproduced in whole or in part in any form without prior written permission from the publisher.

CHILDCRAFT, CHILDCRAFT—THE HOW AND WHY LIBRARY, HOW AND WHY, WORLD BOOK and the GLOBE DEVICE are registered trademarks or trademarks of World Book, Inc.

World Book, Inc.
233 N. Michigan Avenue
Chicago, IL 60601

Previous editions © 2004, 2000, 1996-1993, 1991-1989, 1987-1985 World Book, Inc.; © 1982-1979 World Book-Childcraft International, Inc.; © 1976, 1974-1973, 1971-1968, 1965-1964 Field Enterprises Educational Corporation; International Copyright © 2000, 1996-1993, 1991-1989, 1987-1985, World Book, Inc.; © 1982-1979 World Book-Childcraft International, Inc.; © 1976, 1974-1973, 1971-1968, 1965-1964 Field Enterprises Educational Corporation. All rights reserved.

The Library of Congress has cataloged a previous edition of this title as follows.

Childcraft: the how and why library.
 v. cm.
 Summary: Presents illustrated articles, stories, and poems, grouped thematically in fifteen volumes.
 Includes bibliographical references and indexes.
 Contents: v. 1. Poems and rhymes -- v. 2. Once upon a time -- v. 3. Art around us -- v. 4. The world of animals -- v. 5 The world of plants -- v. 6. Our earth -- v. 7. The universe -- v. 8. How does it happen? -- v. 9. How things work -- v. 10. Shape and numbers -- v. 11. About you -- v. 12. Who we are -- v. 13. See the world -- v. 14. Celebrate! -- v. 15. Guide and index.
 ISBN 0-7166-2203-3 (set)
 1. Children's encyclopedias and dictionaries.
[1. Encyclopedias and dictionaries.]
I. Title: Childcraft. II. World Book, Inc.
AG6 .C48 2004
031--dc21   2003008722

This edition:

ISBN-13: 978-0-7166-2219-2 (set)
ISBN-10: 0-7166-2219-X (set)
ISBN-13: 978-0-7166-2234-5 (Volume 15, Guide and Index)
ISBN-10: 0-7166-2234-3 (Volume 15, Guide and Index)

Printed in China
4 5 6 7 8 9 09 08 07 06

For information on other World Book publications, visit our Web site at **http://www.worldbook.com** or call **1-800 WORLDBK (967-5325)**. For information on sales to schools and libraries, call **1-800-975-3250 (United States)**, or **1-800-837-5365 (Canada)**.

Contents

Get introduced to Childcraft and find out how to use the set to explore the world with your child and supplement your child's schoolwork.

Growth and Development 46

From the formative preschool years to the crucial early school years, parents and teachers play an essential role in children's lives. Learn what to expect during these stages and how to give your child the best possible start in life.

Introduction

This volume of *Childcraft* is for you, the parent, teacher, or adult caregiver of a young child. It is designed to help you to use *Childcraft* and to understand and meet the special needs of young children.

Childcraft is especially designed for children from the preschool years through the early primary grades. During those years, children develop from toddlers, dependent on parents and other adults for help with basic skills, to school-age children who are active learners with friendships outside the home.

The sections of this volume offer help with specific aspects of a young child's growth and development. The first section, "Learning with *Childcraft*," explains the objectives of *Childcraft* and the organization of the set. It provides suggestions for introducing the *Childcraft* set and individual volumes to preschool and school-age children. The suggested activities are designed to capitalize on children's own interests and their curiosity about the world around them. "Learning with *Childcraft*" also contains guides for using the volumes to enrich areas of the school curriculum, such as language and literature, critical thinking, math, science, social studies, and the arts.

The second section, "Growth and Development," outlines the physical, mental, and emotional development of young children. The first part of "Growth and Development" describes the motor skills, social development, and language development of children from 3 to 5 and from 5 to 8 years old, and the kinds of learning experiences that children in each age group need and enjoy. It also offers some helpful ideas about dealing with special needs of children in each age group—for example, coping with the preschooler's fears or tendencies to dawdle, and helping the school-age child learn to travel between home and school safely, handle an allowance, and cope with social problems at school.

The second part of "Growth and Development," titled "For Special Consideration," contains articles about subjects that may affect young children at any time, such as growing, moving, traveling, or coping with the loss of a loved family member, friend, or pet. It also contains articles about special problems that affect only some parents and teachers, such as children's physical disabilities, mental retardation, and behavioral problems. At the end of the section, you will find reprinted a plain text version of *The Convention on Rights of the Child,* adopted by the United Nations in 1989, which outlines the basic needs and rights of children worldwide.

The third section, the Index, is a comprehensive listing of subject-area content for all volumes of *Childcraft.* This index is especially helpful in locating related information on arts, sciences, technology, and growth and development in all of Volumes 1-14. If you are sharing *Childcraft* with a young child, you can use the index to find topics quickly and easily. Or, you can help a child who is reading learn to use the index to look up topics of special interest.

Obviously, no single person and no single book can provide answers and advice on all aspects of growth and development. This volume is designed to give an overall picture of the young child's needs and behavior. The authors and editors hope that you will find it a helpful guide to understanding and meeting the needs of young children.

Learning with *Childcraft*

Childcraft is designed to meet the learning needs of preschool and early school-age children. The organization of the volumes takes into account both how young children learn and what they want to know. It also recognizes that parents, caregivers, and teachers are instrumental in introducing the world of learning to children and making it enjoyable and rewarding.

Getting to Know *Childcraft*

The best kind of learning is fun. Children have a natural curiosity about themselves and their world, and they enjoy satisfying that curiosity. *Childcraft* helps children find answers to their questions and encourages them to explore further and find more questions to answer. It is an exciting companion for an inquisitive child. In addition, *Childcraft* is an ideal assistant for the parent or teacher of any child because it provides accurate information on a wide range of topics in language that children themselves can understand.

Objectives of *Childcraft*

Childcraft is for children. These four words represent the purpose for creating *Childcraft*. The goal of *Childcraft* is to explain ideas clearly and interestingly to children, so as to challenge, stimulate, and create an appetite for more.

The creators of *Childcraft* worked to choose topics of high interest to children from preschool through elementary school years. They chose stories and poems from folk literature, the classics, and the best of today's literature for children. They researched topics in nature, the sciences, the arts, and social studies—topics that parents and teachers consider significant. Then they organized the material in volumes centered around children's interests and filled with simple, direct writing and informative, exciting photography and art.

Childcraft and Children's interests

Childcraft is designed to satisfy both young children's need to know and their need to explore and understand the world of imagination and feelings. Volumes 1 and 2 nourish a child's imagination with the best of children's stories and poems— selections that help children become more aware and understanding of themselves and others. Volumes 3–14 explore the outside world, developing basic concepts and adding supporting information for children. Each volume builds on the child's knowledge and interests and points toward further learning.

In Volumes 3–14, the writers of *Childcraft* have used a style that lets children enjoy the language while learning the facts. The writing is conversational and direct, with a natural rhythm. Unfamiliar words are introduced and explained either in the selection itself or in a glossary at the end of the volume.

The illustrations are colorful and appealing. Children will find charts and diagrams that clarify the text as well as illustrations and photographs that stimulate emotional responses to the stories and poems.

Childcraft and developmental needs

Childcraft is designed both to satisfy children and to meet the needs of parents, teachers, and other caring adults in a child's life. Adults who use *Childcraft* will find a wealth of information, literature, and activities for a range of ages.

This section of the *Guide and Index*, "Learning with *Childcraft*," provides you with an overview of content, together with suggestions for introducing and using specific volumes at home and in the classroom. Two articles that follow, "Introducing *Childcraft* to Children" and "Curriculum enrichment," together with the tables of contents and indexes of the individual volumes, will help you guide children to the books and pages that have the right information.

Organization of *Childcraft*

The first two volumes of *Childcraft* introduce children to literature from all ages and from around the world. In volumes 3–14, children learn about living things, machines and numbers, stars and planets, the arts, the world and its people, and themselves. Volume 15 contains articles on child development for parents and teachers.

In Volumes 3–14, most material is presented as two-page articles. Each of these volumes includes a subject index.

Description of Contents

Volume 1 **Poems and Rhymes**

This volume contains selections to read aloud and share with young children—nursery rhymes, poems, and proverbs. Throughout this volume, you'll find classic Mother Goose rhymes, translated rhymes from many countries and cultures, and many other fun poems to read.

The selections are arranged into five sections—"For Fun," which has a wide variety of subjects; "Things to Know," which introduces the alphabet, counting rhymes, and poems about other concepts; "Animals Only," which focuses on rhymes about animals; "Just Play," which is full of finger rhymes, jump-rope rhymes, and tongue twisters; and "Wise Words," which is a selection of fables and proverbs from around the world.

Volume 2 **Once Upon a Time**

The second volume features selections for children who are beginning to read—fairy tales, folk tales, and stories. Many familiar classics are included, such as "Jack and the Beanstalk," "The Emperor's New Clothes," and "Cinderella," along with examples from many countries, including the African tale "Why Mosquitoes Buzz in People's Ears."

The selections are grouped into three sections—"Fairy Tales," "Folk Tales and Legends," and "Stories and Excerpts."

Volume 3 **Art Around Us**

The third volume encourages children to learn about different forms of art and how to create art with objects they find around them. Throughout this volume, children are enlightened to the possibilities of using odds and ends such as paper clips and flower petals as well as paints, clay, papier mâché, and fabrics to create works of art. They are also introduced to great representatives of the arts—Prokofiev, Shakespeare, Michelangelo and many others.

This volume is arranged in five sections—"Craftwork," "Let's Paint," "Statues and Sculptures," "Music to Your Ears," and "Theater."

Volume 4 **The World of Animals**

Mammals, birds, fish, reptiles, amphibians, and other animals are featured, along with explanations of the characteristics of each group, how animals fit into the web of life, and how animals and people affect each other.

This volume has eight general chapters, including "What Is an Animal?" "Amazing Animals," and "Animals in Danger," as well as five chapters explaining seven different classes of animals.

Volume 5 **The World of Plants**

As well as teaching the facts of plant life, the fifth volume focuses on how important plants are to us— how we use them for food and to make paper, cloth, even buildings and medicine. The text also demonstrates how important it is that people, in turn, should look after the world of plants.

"The Life of a Plant," "Nature's Neighbors," "What Plants Do for Us," "How Does your Garden Grow?" and "Plants Need Help, Too" are the five sections that make up this volume.

Volume 6 **Our Earth**

The sixth book describes the dramatic phenomena of the earth's activities and stimulates children's interest in their own environment.

The volume approaches the subject process by process, describing each topic in a strongly visual manner.

Starting with "Planet Earth," then moving through "Land on the Earth," "Oceans, Lakes, and Rivers," "Air, Wind, and Clouds," and "Weather," Volume 6 leaves us contemplating "Why Protect the Earth?" and "How Can People Protect the Earth?"

Volume 7 **The Universe**

In this book about astronomy, the sun, Earth's moon, and each planet of the solar system are dealt with in detail. Then the text moves beyond the solar system into the stars and galaxies of the universe. The physical aspects of astronomy, the applications of space technology, and research in the field of communications are also discussed.

The five chapters of this volume are "The Sun," "The Moon," "Our Solar System," "The Stars," and "Studying the Universe."

Volume 8 **How Does It Happen?**

This book helps satisfy children's curiosity about basic principles of science. Simple text and generous illustrations help children understand the interaction of matter and energy in the world around them.

Divided into eight sections, including "What Happens with Machines?" and "What Makes Things Move?" this volume also tackles matter, energy, heat and cold, light, sound, and electricity.

Volume 9 How Things Work

The ninth volume applies the concepts discussed in *How Does It Happen?* to everyday tools and machines, giving clear and practical demonstrations of the principles introduced. In addition, this volume underlines the value of raw materials. Children will gain a greater appreciation of the application of science and the importance of technology in our everyday lives.

The five sections in this volume are "Inventions in the Home," which tackles such inventions as refrigerators and computers; "On the Move," which covers machines such as escalators, cars, and rockets; "Signals in the Air," which explores the workings of such inventions as satellites, radios, and television; "Raw Materials," which explains how everyday items from cheese to paper and plastics are made; and "Creating and Designing," which talks about the structures of houses and bridges as well as the functions of robots in manufacturing things.

Volume 10 Shapes and Numbers

This book entertains and challenges young readers with stories, puzzles, games, tricks, and facts about shapes and numbers. It explores such topics as how we can play and work with numbers, and where numbers came from.

The chapters in this volume are "Fun with Shapes," "The Story of Numbers," "Making Numbers Count" "Go Figure!" "More Number Fun" and "Ways of Measuring."

Volume 11 About You

This book answers questions of special interest to young children—questions about how people are alike and different, the parts of the human body and how they work, and what feelings are. Particularly complex subjects are explained in simple language with colorful illustrations to highlight and further clarify the text.

Beginning with "Outside of You," this volume also has chapters called "Inside of You," "Your Senses," "Growing and Changing," "Thoughts and Feelings," and "Taking Care of Yourself."

Volume 12 Who We Are

This volume explores the many likenesses and differences in people and cultures around the world—ways of life, beliefs and customs, food, games, and education.

This book is divided into five sections—"Families and Neighbors," "What Do We Eat?" "What Games Do We Play?" "How Do We Learn Things?" and "How Do We All Get Along?"

Volume 13 See the World

This book tells about the continents, the ways people get around, and how to use maps and plan a trip. In addition, this volume introduces children to some of the most famous places in our world. Castles, natural and historic "wonders of the world," famous skyscrapers, and national monuments, along with many other well-known places, are shown in bright illustrations and photographs that will captivate a young child's imagination.

The six chapters in this volume are "Continents of the World," "How Will You Get There?" "Where in the World?" "Famous Places," "How Do You Find Your Way?" and "Taking a Trip."

Volume 14 Celebrate!

In this book, children learn how people celebrate all over the world and discover that every month of the year there is a celebration somewhere in the world. Children also can look up their birthdays in this volume to find out what famous historical figures were born on the same date.

This book starts with "What's a Celebration?" followed by a chapter for each month of the year, highlighting some of that month's holidays and birthdays.

Volume 15 Guide and Index

This volume for parents and teachers outlines a child's growth and development from birth through the preteen years and explores issues of special concern. The volume includes suggestions for introducing and using *Childcraft*; articles about child development; and suggestions for coping with common illnesses, traveling with young children, and other special circumstances; as well as the general index for the entire series. The sections are "Learning with *Childcraft*," "A Child's Growth and Development from Three Years to Eight," and "Index."

Introducing *Childcraft* to Children

Through using *Childcraft,* children and parents alike come to love and appreciate it as a good friend. It reflects children's interests, recognizes the importance of the relationship between parent and child, and provides a stimulating way to learn.

Childcraft's effectiveness at home depends largely on how it is presented and used. It's important that you get to know *Childcraft* before introducing it to your child. If you browse through each volume, it will be easy for you to share it enthusiastically with your child.

Sharing pictures and stories from *Childcraft* is a natural way to introduce a young child to each volume of the set. These pages offer you suggestions for exploring *Childcraft* as a whole and exploring individual volumes with your child.

Preschool

BIRTH-3. This is the time to introduce *Childcraft* to your children. Set aside 15 or 20 minutes each day to share *Childcraft* with your child. This time period can vary—infants and toddlers have short attention spans, and it's important not to overdo it. Sharing *Childcraft* will help to stimulate an infant's mind and reinforce the toddler's newly acquired ability to talk.

Poems and Rhymes is specially geared to infants and toddlers. Your enthusiastic, animated presentation of rhymes and poems will encourage your child to imitate sounds and actions. With reassurance and guidance, your child can sharpen skills. Counting and action rhymes will help toddlers learn basic counting and language. Encourage your child to join in!

Ages 3-4. The transition to the preschool years is marked by an expanded vocabulary, a longer attention span, and a preoccupation with fantasy and role-playing. A 4-year-old's complete openness to learning makes sharing *Childcraft* a really rewarding experience for both parent and child.

Although most 4-year-olds can't read words, they can "read" pictures to create or re-create their own stories. They love to talk about stories that are read to them. Allow time for your child to respond and question. There's no need to hurry to the end of the story unless your child wants to. Frequent pauses to discuss pictures or passages will enable your child to re-create the story in his or her own way.

Preschoolers enjoy browsing through *Childcraft* on their own, so now is the time to teach your child how to care for books. Your child will try to imitate almost everything you do, so if you treat books with care and respect, your child will quickly learn to treat books and treasured possessions with care.

The bright photos and illustrations in *Childcraft* will stimulate interest. Often, the preschooler will want feedback on the wonders in *Childcraft*. The clear, simple text will help you respond to questions in terms your child will understand.

School Age

Ages 5-7. As soon as children learn to read, their involvement with *Childcraft* will broaden, and they will start to read alone. Indeed, they will begin to explore more and more of *Childcraft* on their own.

During their first year of school, most children will continue to need some adult help in exploring *Childcraft*. In the second or third year, however, they will begin to make more use of the book without parental help. The first two volumes hold material for the reading level of this important age group. This is also an age when children become intensely curious about themselves, so the volume *About You* becomes especially important.

Place the books where your child can see them and reach them easily. Make it clear that your child can use these books at any time, but also is responsible for looking after them. This, too, is part of the learning process.

Free access to *Childcraft* will bolster a growing sense of competence and independence. Children will also find in *Childcraft* references to material they come across at school. If they've enjoyed *Childcraft* in their early years, they will easily develop the habit of checking *Childcraft* for information they need.

Ages 7–10. Children are often intrigued by differences in lifestyles. The volumes entitled *Who We Are* and *See the World* show the different ways people live, in what kinds of houses they live, what they eat, and fascinating examples of customs around the world. So children can go off on any tangent they choose—one element will always lead to another. They will learn that there is no limit to knowledge, if they are encouraged to pursue it.

Since most of the volumes relate to school subjects, *Childcraft* is a superb home reference library for children in grade school. Children will find material in *Childcraft* that will help them complete school assignments. *Childcraft* will help with homework problems and will still be a pleasurable experience.

During the grade-school years, children's attention tends to focus on other children. The codes, styles, and expectations of other children in the same age group will determine a great deal of each child's behavior. The familiar practice of sharing *Childcraft* with a parent may shift to sharing *Childcraft* with a friend or group of friends. The important thing is that *Childcraft* should remain a source of enjoyment and information.

Volume 1 *Poems and Rhymes* and Volume 2 *Once Upon a Time*

Reading to your child is a wonderful way to share a close, loving relationship, for it is a time of pleasure for both of you. Your child is learning that a book holds a world of wonder and enjoyment.

At the same time, your child is learning that those strange black lines on the pages are the source of the words you speak and that someday he or she will be able to read those words, too. He or she is also discovering that you are reading from left to right and from top to bottom. And think about the pictures your child studies so intently. The realization that the flat apple on the page represents a real, rounded apple he or she can hold is an enormous leap in comprehension.

Story time provides opportunities to improve vocabulary and develop readiness for reading. Many studies have shown the connection between reading to children and their success in learning basic reading skills. So, as you read, talk about the story and answer your child's questions about letters, sounds, and words.

Before you read any story or poem to your child, read it, or at least skim it, yourself. Ask yourself: Will this interest my child? Will he or she understand what is happening? What unfamiliar words or ideas might I have to explain? Is this a good bedtime story, or should I read it at some other time?

Preschool

Activity 1. No child is too young to be read to. Many educators recommend reading short, simple rhymes to infants a few weeks old. Read from the "For Fun" section of *Poems and Rhymes*. Your baby will respond to the rhythm of the words and the sound of your voice. Play with your child's hands, fingers, or toes as your read "Pat-a-Cake" or "This Little Piggy." This is fun for your baby and will soon draw smiles. These happy responses establish patterns for later learning.

Activity 2. Introduce Volume 1 to your child by reading one or two nursery rhymes. Put your finger under the words as you read them to help your child make an association between spoken and written words. Repeat each rhyme so that your child can learn part or all of it and recite it with you. If there are pictures illustrating the rhyme, point them out and talk about them with your child. In later sessions, as your child's attention span increases, go on to the other types of poetry and to the shorter tales and stories.

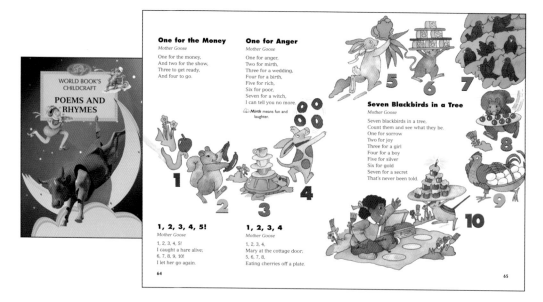

Activity 3. Continue to read nursery rhymes to your toddler, but try some simple stories in *Once Upon a Time,* too, like "Mother, Mother, I Want Another" or "It's My Birthday." If necessary, shorten the tales and use your own words to tell simplified versions that still match the pictures. As you read, point to characters and objects in the pictures.

Activity 4. For children 3 to 5, you will be able to read complete stories. Most children in this age group will enjoy a short folk tale or fairy tale, such as "Why the Bear Has a Stumpy Tail" from *Once Upon a Time* or "The Lion and the Mouse" from *Poems and Rhymes.*

This is also a good time to use the section "Things to Know" in *Poems and Rhymes.* Here are rhymes about many of the concepts you'll want your child to understand before school begins—the alphabet, numbers from 1 to 10, days of the week, colors, and good manners.

School Age

Activity 1. Now is the time to look for stories with a more complex turn of plot, such as "Cinderella," "Jack and the Beanstalk," and "Why Mosquitoes Buzz in People's Ears." If a story is too long for one sitting, read just a few pages at a time. Look for poems, too, that match your child's special interests.

Activity 2. At 7, most children can read easy stories. This, however, does not mean that you should stop reading aloud. Reading aloud gives you a chance to whet your child's appetite for some of the great classics for children in *Once Upon a Time.* After your child has begun reading, help him or her begin using *Poems and Rhymes* independently, even while you continue reading aloud. For example, read to your child one of the long story poems, such as "Three Little Kittens" on pages 96–97, "The Fox Went Out on a Chilly Night" on pages 120–125, and "The Owl and the Pussycat" by Edward Lear on pages 130–131. Then point out that most of the poems in *Poems and Rhymes* are much shorter than the one you read and that your child may be able to read some of them. Turn to "Things to Know" on pages 52–91. Point out that almost all the words in these poems are easy to read. Encourage your child to try reading the poems.

Activity 3. If your child is developing strong reading skills, take time to look through Volume 1 with him or her. Note that this is where the nursery rhymes and other poems are found. Also look through *Once Upon a Time* with your child and point out the easiest stories, such as "The Little Red Hen," on pages 90–92, and "Mother, Mother, I Want Another," by Maria Polushkin, on pages 140–147. Let your child choose a short poem and read it to you. Encourage your child to read other poems and stories alone.

Activity 4. Browse through the stories in *Once Upon a Time* with your child and have him or her predict from the pictures what each story is about. Ask which stories look most interesting and why. Help your child find stories that are comfortable reading and choose one to read. Have your child read the first paragraph or so aloud to you and finish reading the story independently. Encourage your child to go on to others.

Activity 5. Your child may be interested in stories in *Once Upon a Time* that are beyond his or her reading level. Don't forget that even though children are reading on their own, they still enjoy being read to. When your child seems interested in a story but cannot read it alone, read it aloud slowly, following the text with your finger so your child can follow along.

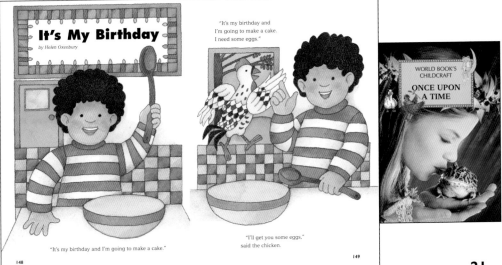

Volume 3 *Art Around Us*

Preschool

Activity 1. Prepare to introduce Volume 3, *Art Around Us,* by previewing pages 12–13 to learn what types of materials are needed for the easy crafts and activities in this book. Then, with your child, look through the pages and choose one of the projects. Help your child with the directions if necessary. Then talk about what materials to collect for other projects, where to store them, where to work on the projects, and how to clean up.

Activity 2. Pick a chapter in the book in which your child would be especially interested. Flip through the pages of this chapter with your child, looking at and discussing the pictures. Talk to your child about examples of these art forms in everyday life, such as a painting or figurine in your home. Talk about a puppet show your child saw and compare it to the theater.

School Age

Activity 1. Read through the chapter called "Music to Your Ears" with your child and make a list of the types of music your child finds most interesting. Then take your child to your local library and check out recordings of these types and some others. Listen to the music at home together and talk about what your child likes in each style.

Activity 2. Read about puppets with your child on pages 166–169. Then help your child make one or two puppets using the instructions on pages 170–173. Ask your child to think of a simple story to act out as a puppet show.

Getting Crafty

To do all the crafts in this chapter, you will need lots of materials. Some things you will need for only one project. But other things you will use again and again.

It is a good idea to collect the materials listed on page 13 and keep them in a large cardboard box. Then you will have the materials you need to work with.

Where will you find your materials? You may have to buy some at a craft store. But you can start your collecting at home and outside. Remember to get permission before you add something to your collection. And be careful when handling sharp objects.

WORLD BOOK'S CHILDCRAFT
ART AROUND US

Craft materials to collect
- rubber bands
- tracing paper
- bowls of different sizes
- cardboard
- clear tape
- crayons
- glue
- flowers
- leaves
- food coloring
- heavyweight and lightweight paper in different colors
- magazines
- markers
- masking tape
- newspaper
- open-weave canvas
- pencils
- pieces of cloth
- a ruler
- scissors
- streamers
- string
- tissue paper
- wax paper
- embroidery hoop
- embroidery needle
- embroidery thread

12

Animals Eat

All plants and all animals need food. Most plants make their own food from light, water, and **substances** in the ground and air. But animals cannot make their own food. They must eat plants or other animals to live.

Different kinds of animals eat in different kinds of ways. A chameleon (kuh MEE lee uhn) flips out its sticky tongue and catches insects. A lammergeier, a type of vulture, uses its sharp claws and hooked beak to tear its food.

A butterfly has a mouthpart like a built-in straw. It's called a proboscis (proh BAHS ihs). The butterfly keeps its proboscis rolled up until it gets hungry. Then it unrolls its proboscis, puts it into a flower, and sucks up sweet nectar.

African lammergeier

butterfly

A ground squirrel has strong teeth for cracking nuts and seeds. It carries food home in its cheeks and "squirrels" it away.

A baleen whale fills its mouth with seawater. The water is full of tiny plants and animals. The whale lets the water run out of its mouth. Then it swallows the plants and animals that remain.

South American giant anteater

raccoon

KNOW IT ALL What's for dinner? Animals can be grouped by what they eat. Some animals eat only plants. They are called herbivores. Herbivores include cattle, sheep, and squirrels. Animals that eat only other animals are called carnivores. Carnivores include lions, foxes, and snakes. Animals that eat both plants and animals are called omnivores. Omnivores include bears, raccoons, hogs, and human beings. What do you think animals that eat only insects are called? Right! Insectivores. Anteaters and hedgehogs are insectivores.

king cobra

12

golden-mantled ground squirrel

WORLD BOOK'S CHILDCRAFT
THE WORLD OF ANIMALS

Volume 4 *The World of Animals*

Preschool

Activity 1. Explain that Volume 4, *The World of Animals,* shows how animals belong in groups. Turn to the table of contents and read the eight chapter titles to your child. Then invite your child to choose one chapter to find out what the title means. Turn to the first two pages, read them, and talk about the illustration. Encourage your child to talk about what he or she sees on these pages.

Activity 2. Point out many other colorful and informative pictures throughout the volume. Encourage your child to look at the pictures just for fun and to find out about animals of all types. Also encourage your child to bring any questions he or she may have to you.

School Age

Activity 1. Explain that people who study animals put animals that are alike into groups. Explain that several chapters in *The World of Animals* tell about different animal groups. Read the title and introduction of any chapter opener to your child. Invite your child to choose a chapter and to browse through the articles and pictures independently.

Activity 2. Ask your child to name a favorite animal. Use the index to find pages of *The World of Animals* that discuss or illustrate the animals. If there is a picture, help your child read the caption.

Invite your child to name other favorite animals. Use the index to help your child find the pages that have pictures or text about them.

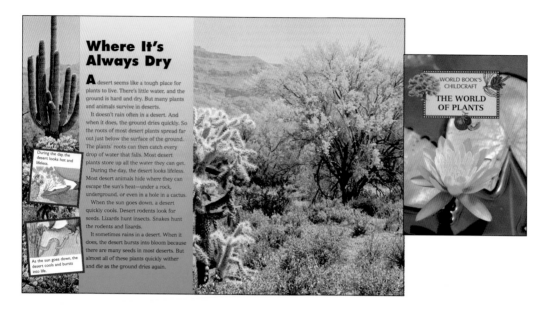

Where It's Always Dry

A desert seems like a tough place for plants to live. There's little water, and the ground is hard and dry. But many plants and animals survive in deserts.

It doesn't rain often in a desert. And when it does, the ground dries quickly. So the roots of most desert plants spread far out just below the surface of the ground. The plants' roots can then catch every drop of water that falls. Most desert plants store up all the water they can get.

During the day, the desert looks lifeless. Most desert animals hide where they can escape the sun's heat—under a rock, underground, or even in a hole in a cactus.

When the sun goes down, a desert quickly cools. Desert rodents look for seeds. Lizards hunt insects. Snakes hunt the rodents and lizards.

It sometimes rains in a desert. When it does, the desert bursts into bloom because there are many seeds in most deserts. But almost all of these plants quickly wither and die as the ground dries again.

During the day, the desert looks hot and lifeless.

As the sun goes down, the desert cools and bursts into life.

WORLD BOOK'S CHILDCRAFT
THE WORLD OF PLANTS

Volume 5 *The World of Plants*

Preschool

Activity 1. Read the title of Volume 5, *The World of Plants,* and explain that the book is about plants of all kinds. Look through the volume for a plant that your child is familiar with. Have your child look at the picture as you read the text. Let your child browse through the book to enjoy the pictures.

Activity 2. Introduce *The World of Plants* as a reference source. Explain that the book tells about all kinds of plants. Look through the book and point out some of the most interesting plants. Encourage your child to look at the pictures in the rest of the book for fun. If your child has questions about the pictures, read some of the text to find answers.

School Age

Activity 1. Turn to one of the four-page articles in the chapter "Nature's Neighbors" on pages 54–87. Read the pages with your child and look at and talk about the pictures, then read the text. Let your child look through the rest of the book and use pictures, captions, and titles to preview the content.

Activity 2. If you have a globe or map of the world, use it as you and your child look through *The World of Plants*. Turn to the article on pages 156–157. Have your child choose a favorite. Then find its location on the globe or map. Point out where you live and the land and water between you and the place your child picked. Discuss how you would get there.

Volume 6 *Our Earth*

Preschool

Activity 1. Some topics in *Our Earth* address questions in every child's early life, such as "What makes the wind blow?" or "Why is the sky blue?" *Our Earth* answers some of these questions.

Introduce *Our Earth* in short sessions. Let your child find a two-page article with an interesting picture. Read the title and ask your child what the picture shows. Then read the article aloud or explain it simply. Limit the activity to 10 minutes.

Activity 2. Let your child look at pictures in the book whenever he or she feels like it and bring questions about them to you for explanations.

School Age

Activity 1. Your child may be ready to read picture labels and captions. Turn to a page with an easy-to-read caption, such as page 10, 77, 80, or 139. After you talk with your child about the illustration, read the caption aloud. Then encourage your child to read it. Compliment your child for correct or approximate readings. Let your child try reading other captions.

Activity 2. Encourage independent reading by helping your child do an experiment, such as "What Is Air Made Of?" (pages 108–109) or "How Does Air Push?" (pages 110–111). With your child, talk about the pictures, read the text, and work the experiment together.

Volume 7 *The Universe*

Preschool

Activity 1. This volume deals with the sun, moon, and stars as well as the solar system, space, and space travel. Introduce *The Universe* by sharing such information as "Why Does the Sun Disappear at Night?" (pages 18–19), "Why Does the Moon Shine?" (pages 46–47), or "What Are Stars?" (pages 100–101). Look at the pictures with your child and read the article or explain as much information as your child wants to know.

Activity 2. Ask your child to name some things the sun does, such as that it rises and sets, gives off light and makes things warm. Then look at the pictures for "Why Is the Sun Important?" (pages 14–17) and read the text or explain it simply. Use the pictures to follow energy from the sun to plants, animals, and people.

School Age

Activity 1. With your child, compare the photographs of the sun (page 11) and moon (page 40.) Talk about the two photos: Does the sun look as hard and rocky as the moon? Does the moon look as hot as the sun? Then have your child find a photo of a planet in Chapter 3, "Our Solar System." Talk about whether the planet might be hot or cold, rocky or made of softer things, like water or clouds. Then read about the planet with your child.

Activity 2. Read "Star Pictures" (pages 108–109) with your child. Then let your child choose and read some of the "Star Stories" (pages 110–113). With your child, look for some of the constellations mentioned in "Finding Star Pictures (pages 114–117).

Volume 8 *How Does It Happen?*

Preschool

Activity 1. Introduce Volume 8, *How Does It Happen?,* to your child by reading "The Fire Bringer" on pages 104–111. Talk about fire with your child, its many uses as well as its dangers.

Activity 2. Read "Energy from Movement" (pages 66–67) to your child and talk about how making something move gives it energy. Let your child think of some examples, such as pushing a swing, throwing a ball, or pushing a stroller. Then let your child try the domino activity (page 66) and see how the energy from pushing one domino travels down the whole row.

School Age

Activity 1. Read "Hard, Wet, and Invisible" (pages 58–59) with your child. Let your child name some familiar things that are solid, liquid, and gas. Then invite your child to read some of the riddles in "Mealtime Matter" (pages 60–63) and name the foods described.

Activity 2. Help your child make the tin-can telephone described on pages 146–147. After building and using the "phone," read the text on pages 138–145 with your child about sound and how it travels. Talk about the vibrations of the string, which take the sound from one can to the other.

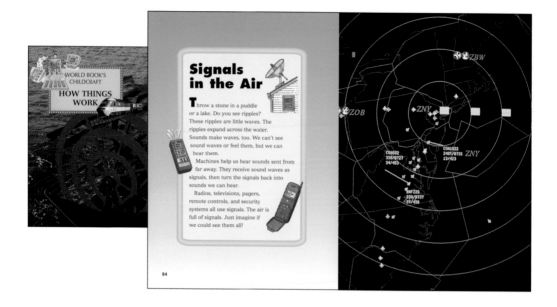

Volume 9 *How Things Work*

Preschool

Activity 1. Choose an easy (level 1) project in Volume 9, *How Things Work,* and collect the materials for it. Then read the title of the book and look through it with your child to see what it is about. Look at the project, read the directions, and do the project together. Talk about just as much of the principle—for example, wind, power, or heat—as you think your child will understand.

Activity 2. Read "Great Idea!" (pages 12–13) in Chapter 1, "Inventions in the Home," to your child. Let your child look through the chapter and find pictures of things people use at home. Then ask your child to think of a new invention to use at home, draw a picture of it, and explain what it does.

School Age

Activity 1. This activity will give your child practice in grouping and classifying. With your child, look through Chapter 2, "On the Move," and find pictures of things that move on land, in water, in the air, and underground. Then let your child name other categories, such as "machines that move people" and "machines that move things," and find some examples of each.

Activity 2. Read the introduction to Chapter 3, "Signals in the Air" (pages 84–85) with your child. Help your child think of some things that work by using signals. Then look through the chapter for examples. Let your child choose one that looks interesting and read the article about it alone or with your help.

Volume 10 *Shapes and Numbers*

Preschool

Activity 1. Introduce Volume 10, *Shapes and Numbers,* by reading one of the stories included in the volume, such as "The Farmer's Square" (pages 20–23) or "The Foolish Millionaire and the Clever Girl" (pages 122–125).

Activity 2. Play "Shape Tangle" (from pages 30–31) with your child. Not only is this game good for teaching shapes, but it also helps your child learn body parts and learn *left* and *right*. Have your child help you make the shapes. As you cut them out, tell your child their names. If just two of you play, take turns being the "caller." Play slowly and encourage your child to think before moving. If your child makes a mistake, give gentle encouragement and help to get it right.

School Age

Activity 1. With your child, work out the answers to your choice of these puzzlers in Volume 10: "Disappearing Squares" (pages 18–19); "Polyominoes" (pages 24–25); and "The Magic Number in Your Name" (pages 96–97).

Activity 2. Explain that *Shapes and Numbers* tells about many ways to think about and work with numbers. Read the table of contents, then turn to one or more of these lessons to explore some math concepts in simple terms: "What's the Biggest Number" (pages 106–107), "The Magic of Multiplication" (pages 110–111), and "What Is Measuring?" (pages 158–159). Depending on your child's reading ability, read the text aloud or help him or her to read.

The Farmer's Square

Long ago, there was a farmer whose land was in the shape of a square. Each side of the square was exactly 100 paces long.

One day, a tired, dusty man knocked at the farmer's door and asked for something to eat. The kind farmer gave him a nice lunch.

After the man had eaten, he said, "Farmer, I am your king! As a reward for your kindness, you may double the size of your land. But after you add the new land, your farm must still be in the shape of a square."

The farmer was overjoyed. He went out at once to **measure** his new land and put a fence around it.

At first the farmer thought the sides of the new square should be 200 paces long—twice as long as the sides of the old square. But this plan didn't work. The square he measured was four times as big as his old farm!

21

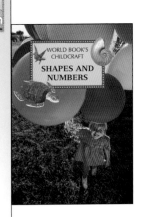

WORLD BOOK'S CHILDCRAFT

SHAPES AND NUMBERS

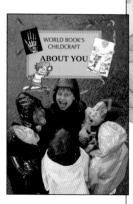

Within the cropped magazine image, the following text appears:

What Happens When You Get Sick?

Do your parents tell you to cover your nose and mouth when you sneeze? That's because when you sneeze, tiny drops of fluid spray out of your mouth. Tiny germs travel in that fluid and can make other people sick too.

Have you had chickenpox or measles, a cold, an ear infection, or the flu? If so, your body was under attack!

When you get sick, tiny germs called viruses (VY ruhs uhz) or bacteria (bak TEER ee uh) attack your body. Some of these germs travel from person to person in the drops of fluid that shoot out of the mouth during a sneeze or cough. Some

are spread in food and water. These germs can make you feel sick.

Luckily your body fights back. And sometimes medicine helps your body fight the germs.

After you have been sick with certain illnesses, your body remembers the germs. If one of the germs tries to attack again, your body destroys it as soon as it enters your body. That's why you usually get some illnesses, like chickenpox, only once.

You can get some illnesses, like colds and the flu, over and over again. This is because there are so many kinds of cold and flu viruses. If a new virus invades your body, your body does not know that virus, and so you get sick.

146   147

Volume 11 *About You*

Preschool

Activity 1. Explain that Volume 11, *About You,* is about growing and taking care of oneself. Turn to "Thoughts and Feelings" on pages 114–143. Look at and talk about the photographs that show activities, moods, emotions, relationships with friends and family members, and curiosity about the future.

Activity 2. The first half of "Growing and Changing" (pages 92–101) is useful for answering the typical question, "Where did I come from?" The pictures illustrate the development of a baby and the life of a newborn infant, and the text gives enough information to satisfy a child's curiosity. Read and talk about this section with your child when you feel the time is right.

School Age

Activity 1. Read and talk about a high-interest article, such as "Your Growing Bones" (pages 102–103), "Families" (pages 108–111), or "What Happens When You Get Sick?" (pages 146–147). Talk about the article with your child and relate it to his or her own life.

Activity 2. If your child is interested in learning about parts of the body, give him or her a preview of the contents of Volume 11. Point out sections about muscles and bones, the respiratory system, the heart and circulatory system, the digestive system, the brain and nervous system, the sensory organs, and so on. Look at some of the pictures together. Read together and talk about any text that interests your child.

Volume 12 *Who We Are*

Preschool

Activity 1. Volume 12, *Who We Are,* is packed with colorful pictures that a preschooler can enjoy. Open the book to pages 4–5. Read page 5 aloud or reword the text in simpler language. Briefly discuss the pictures on page 4 with your child. Explain that the rest of the book tells more about how people around the world do things. Encourage your child to look through the book to see how people live, eat, play, learn, and enjoy life.

Activity 2. Pick a chapter with familiar activities, such as "What Games Do We Play?" Talk about what the people in the pictures are doing, and let your child guess what the chapter is about. Read the captions of pictures that interest your child. Then let your child browse through the book.

School Age

Activity 1. *Who We Are* discusses food, games, toys, education, and other aspects of many cultures. Choose an interesting article, read it with your child, and talk about the pictures. Children sometimes reject or laugh at an unfamiliar way of life. Your acceptance of other people's ways will help interest your child in learning more. Encourage your child to look through the volume.

Activity 2. Use a globe or map when you introduce *Who We Are*. Look at pictures with your child, pointing out the names of countries. Find the countries on the globe or map. Help your child understand that people in different places do things in different ways. Help your child read an interesting article and locate the countries in the article on the globe or map.

On the Playground

Sidewalk games are fun! The names may change, but the games are pretty much the same on playgrounds, sidewalks, and fields all over the world.

Do you play hopscotch? Children all over the world play it. In China, hopscotch is called *Gat Fei Gei,* which means "One-Foot Jumping Flying Machine." In Italy, it's called the *Bell.* In Austria, it's the *Temple.* In Myanmar, children squat with hands on their hips as they jump the squares.

Hopscotch games come in all shapes and sizes. Some have 8 squares in a straight line. Others have as many as 20 squares in the shape of a snail's shell.

Hopscotch is a popular sidewalk game all over the world.

These children in Mexico are playing a game of hopscotch.

Outside a monastery in India, children play hopscotch together.

80

WORLD BOOK'S CHILDCRAFT
WHO WE ARE

Wonders of Long Ago

Did you know that there are monuments, tombs, and huge walls that were built hundreds or even thousands of years ago? Sometimes only small parts, or ruins, of these places remain. But you can still visit them today.

In England, tourists and scientists alike are amazed by Stonehenge, a group of huge, rough-cut stones set in circles. Scientists believe that ancient people built Stonehenge as a gathering place. Much of the monument is gone, but scientists think that when it was first built, an earth wall about 320 feet (98 meters) across circled it. Thirty blocks of gray sandstone stood like guards 13 1/2 feet (4 meters) above the ground.

Ancient peoples built Stonehenge, in England, more than 3,500 years ago.

Another wonder from long ago is the Great Pyramid at Giza in Egypt. Pyramids were built by Egyptians about 4,500 years ago as tombs for their kings. The Great Pyramid contains more than 2 million stone blocks.

The pyramids of Egypt at Giza were one of the Seven Wonders of the Ancient World.

102   103

Volume 13 *See the World*

Preschool

Activity 1. Volume 13, *See the World,* introduces places of historic significance and natural beauty. Since young children have little sense of the past or of faraway places, try to introduce the book with places that exist now, without emphasizing their location. Read about a place of interest with your child and talk about the picture(s).

Activity 2. Bring out similarities and differences between a place in the book and a place that is familiar to your child. For example, if a picture shows a cathedral, compare it to a church building near your home or one that you have visited together. If some of the stories you and your child have read are set in places mentioned in the text, look at the picture together to find things the stories mentioned.

School Age

Activity 1. Explain that the book is organized by themes. Read several titles from the table of contents and invite your child to choose a part in which he or she is interested. Look through the pages together, reading the titles and captions. Encourage your child to look at other parts of the book independently.

Activity 2. Show your child the index of *See the World* and explain the purpose of an index. Ask your child to name different kinds of places, such as a river, castle, or mountain. If those places are listed, look up and read about them with your child.

Volume 14 *Celebrate!*

Preschool

Activity 1. Use a home calendar to introduce Volume 14, *Celebrate!* Explain that this book tells about the days of the year and what makes them special. Point out today's date on your home calendar, and turn to the chapter about the month. Compare the two calendars. Explain that the one in the book shows birthdays of famous people. Find today's date and read the name(s). Next, find the calendar in the book that lists your child's birthday. Read the names of famous people with the same birthday.

Activity 2. When your family observes a holiday, look at its text and pictures with your child. For birthdays, use the calendar to learn which famous people share the same birthday.

School Age

Activity 1. Introduce *Celebrate!* by explaining its organization according to the months of the year. Then choose one month—the one with your child's birthday or another month with special significance—and look at the calendar and read one or more articles. Encourage your child to look at the book each month to find some special days.

Activity 2. You can show a child who is reading fairly independently how to use *Celebrate!* for reference. After looking at the month-by-month organization, turn to the index. Read through some of the topics and turn to the pages listed. Help your child see that he or she can use both the table of contents and the index to find information about a date, ceremony, or event.

Curriculum Enrichment

The following sections relate *Childcraft* to typical preschool, primary, and lower intermediate-grade curriculum objectives in eight subject areas: (1) Language Arts and Literature; (2) Critical Thinking Skills; (3) Mathematics; (4) Science; (5) Social Studies; (6) Creative Arts; (7) Self-Understanding, Health, and Safety; and (8) Careers. Each section includes suggested introductory activities.

For additional topics, look in the index at the back of this book.

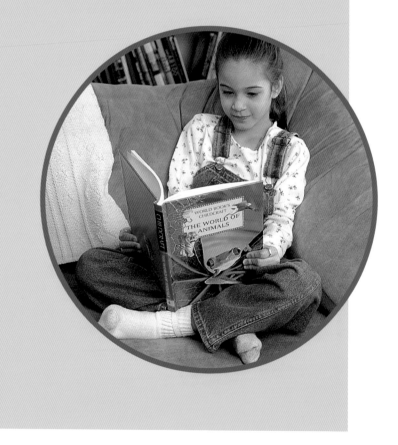

Language Arts and Literature

Listening

For information. (Grades 2–4) Read a short factual article about an animal or animal behavior (Volume 4), plant life (Volume 5), or a holiday (Volume 14). Then ask several questions that require children to recall details in the article.

For pleasure. (Grades 1–2) Read a story in Volume 2 and have children draw, color, or paint illustrations of the characters or events in the story.

Speaking

In discussions. (Grades 1–4) Read a selection from Volume 12 that discusses a custom or way of life of a different country. Ask the children to tell how this behavior is like or different from what is done in their own cultures.

Making presentations. (Grades 2–4) Challenge a child to read one of the math puzzles or games in Volume 10. Invite him or her to present the puzzle to other children and, if the other children cannot figure it out, to explain the answer or "trick" involved.

Poetry and choral reading. (Preschool) Teach one or more poems in Volume 1 to the children until they can say the poem(s) in unison. Encourage good pronunciation and appropriate expression.

(Grades 1–4) Invite the children to choose favorite poems from Volume 1 and read them to the group. As needed, help individual children select poems at their reading level or prepare the poem for presentation.

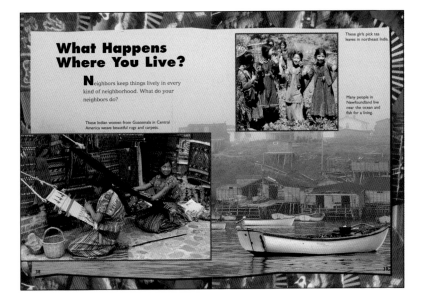

Dramatics. (Grades 2–4) After the children have read or heard one of the stories in Volume 2, have them break into small groups to act out the story in front of the class.

Vocabulary

Recognizing context clues.
(Grades 2–4) When you are reading a passage that explains a new term in context or with the help of an illustration, point out the new term. Reread the passage and have the children raise their hands when they hear its meaning explained.

Using the glossary. (Grades 2–4)
Distribute Volumes 3–14 to children. Have them turn to the glossaries of their volumes. Explain that the glossary for each book is like a dictionary for words that are especially important in that book. Have the children compare words listed in different volumes.

Writing

Mechanics (prose and poetry).
(Grades 1–2) Use selections in *Poems and Rhymes* (Volume 1) and *Once Upon a Time* (Volume 2) to point out differences in poetry and stories, such as the use of lines or paragraphs, the use of capital letters, and the length.

Creative writing. (Grades 2–4)
Read stories to the children from *Once Upon a Time*. Ask the children to write stories of their own.

Report writing. (Grades 2–4) Use
articles in Volumes 3–14 as models of nonfiction writing. For example, read "Feathers and Wings" (Volume 4, pages 56–57) and ask such questions as "What does the first paragraph tell you?" "How do the next paragraphs help you understand the first paragraph?" and "Is there any other information you need to understand this?"

"Of course," Sun answered. "The party is just beginning!" So more Water entered the house. Now it poured through the windows as well as the doors.

Soon, Water was high enough to cover a person's head. Again Water asked Sun if he and his family could keep coming in. "Of course!" Sun said again.

Finally, there was so much Water in the house that Sun and Moon had to sit on the roof. "Should we keep coming in?" Water asked.

Sun and Moon were having too much fun to say no. More of Water and more sea creatures poured into the house, until finally it was completely full. Sun and Moon had to go up into the sky, and that is where they have lived ever since.

104

105

Reading

Reading readiness. (Preschool) Reinforce your teaching of rhyming sounds by reading some rhymes in Volume 1. Read each poem up to the concluding rhyme, and let the children provide the last word.

Reading in content areas. (Grades 2–4) Encourage children to read selections in Volumes 3 through 14 for information and to use their findings in making oral or written reports, posters, or art projects.

Reading techniques—using illustrations. (Preschool, Grades 1–2) Encourage children to look through Volumes 3 through 14 for the information they can glean from pictures. Suggest that they use "Show and Tell" time to tell about the pictures they have examined.

Snowy Morning
by Lilian Moore

Wake
gently this morning
to a different day.
Listen.
There is no bray
of buses,
no brake growls,
no siren howls and
no horns
blow.
There is only
the silence
of a city
hushed
by snow.

Bray means loud, harsh sound, like a donkey makes.

My Zipper Suit
by Marie Louise Allen

My zipper suit is bunny-brown—
The top zips up, the legs zip down.
I wear it every day.
My daddy brought it out from town.
Zip it up, and zip it down,
And hurry out to play!

Thaw
by Eunice Tietjens

The snow is soft,
and how it squashes!
"Galumph, galumph!"
go my galoshes.

Cynthia in the Snow
by Gwendolyn Brooks

IT SUSHES.
It hushes
The loudness in the road.
It flitter-twitters,
And laughs away from me.
It laughs a lovely whiteness,
And whitely whirs away,
To be
Some otherwhere,
Still white as milk or shirts.
So beautiful it hurts.

The Mitten Song
by Marie Louise Allen

"Thumbs in the thumb-place,
Fingers all together!"
This is the song
We sing in mitten-weather.
When it is cold,
It doesn't matter whether
Mittens are wool,
Or made of finest leather.
This is the song
We sing in mitten-weather:
"Thumbs in the thumb-place,
Fingers all together!"

38   39

Reading techniques—using titles and captions. (Grades 1–4) Ask questions about a selection whose answers can be found in the title or picture caption(s). Allow children a short time to find the answers, and let them tell what led them to a particular answer.

Literature appreciation

Awareness of style and word choice in poetry or prose. (Grades 1–4) Use poems in Volume 1 to compare and contrast two types of writing or writing styles. For example, read Lilian Moore's "Snowy Morning" (page 38), "Thaw" by Eunice Tietjens (page 38), and "Cynthia in the Snow" by Gwendolyn Brooks (page 39). Ask about the different ways the poets describe snow. Ask the children to describe it in their own words.

(Grades 2–4) After children have read or heard a selection from *Childcraft,* discuss the words the author uses and their connotations. For example, in "Why Bear Has a Stumpy Tail" (Volume 2, pages 106–107), the fox is described as "slinking along." Ask children whether they think "slinking" is a good descriptive word and how it makes them feel about the fox when they hear it. Ask children to think of other words that might be used in place of "slinking."

Critical Thinking Skills

Classification

(Grades 1–2) Read titles of the volumes with the children. Invite them to tell what kinds of things they might read about in each one.

(Grades 2–4) Ask children to look at the tables of contents of different volumes and discuss how the topics are grouped in each one.

Drawing comparisons and contrasts

(Grades 1–4) Help children use articles about animals and plants in volumes 4 and 5 to discover characteristics of specific types and differences between types. Read the articles to the class, or have children read them, and then discuss the information. Have small groups of children collect magazine and newspaper photographs illustrating some characteristics of a certain group of animals or plants, or have them make charts showing differences between groups.

Separating fact from opinion

(Grades 2–4) Read a legend or myth about nature, such as "Myths About the Moon" (Volume 7, pages 42–45), and a factual explanation, "What Is the Moon Like?" (Volume 7, pages 54–55). Then ask children to list the facts about the moon and the ideas people have had about the moon in two separate columns on an experience chart or the chalkboard.

Logical reasoning

(Grades 2–4) Challenge children to try some activities and puzzles in Volume 10 that require reasoning, such as classifying objects (pages 76–77, 78–79). Have them suggest some categories of objects they can use for a scavenger hunt inside or outdoors.

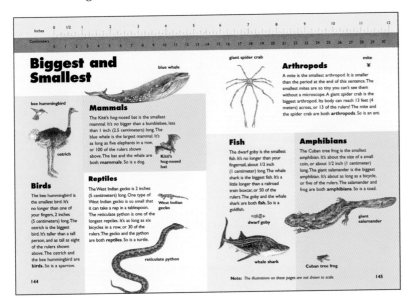

Biggest and Smallest

Mammals
The Kitti's hog-nosed bat is the smallest mammal. It's no bigger than a bumblebee, less than 1 inch (2.5 centimeters) long. The blue whale is the largest mammal. It's as long as five elephants in a row, or 100 of the rulers shown above. The bat and the whale are both **mammals**. So is a dog.

Birds
The bee hummingbird is the smallest bird. It's no longer than your fingers, 2 inches (5 centimeters) long. The ostrich is the biggest bird. It's taller than a tall person, and as tall as eight of the rulers shown above. The ostrich and the bee hummingbird are **birds**. So is a sparrow.

Reptiles
The West Indian gecko is 2 inches (5 centimeters) long. One type of West Indian gecko is so small that it can take a nap in a tablespoon. The reticulate python is one of the longest reptiles. It's as long as six bicycles in a row, or 30 of the rulers. The gecko and the python are both **reptiles**. So is a turtle.

Arthropods
A mite is the smallest arthropod. It is smaller than the period at the end of this sentence. The smallest mites are so tiny you can't see them without a microscope. A giant spider crab is the biggest arthropod. Its body can reach 13 feet (4 meters) across, or 13 of the rulers! The mite and the spider crab are both **arthropods**. So is an ant.

Fish
The dwarf goby is the smallest fish. It's no longer than your fingernail, about 1/2 inch (1 centimeter) long. The whale shark is the biggest fish. It's a little longer than a railroad train boxcar, or 50 of the rulers. The goby and the whale shark are both **fish**. So is a goldfish.

Amphibians
The Cuban tree frog is the smallest amphibian. It's about the size of a small coin, or about 1/2 inch (1 centimeter) long. The giant salamander is the biggest amphibian. It's about as long as a bicycle, or five of the rulers. The salamander and frog are both **amphibians**. So is a toad.

Note: The illustrations on these pages are not drawn to scale.

144   145

Mathematics

Numbers and numerals

(Grades 1–2) Read articles from "The Story of Numbers" in Volume 10, such as pages 46–47, 48–49, and 50–51. Then invite children to count small objects, such as beads or buttons, as described on pages 50–51 and use markers or make marks on paper for each group of 10.

(Grades 2–4) Read the articles about numerals and number systems in Volume 10. Then have the children form groups, and have each group show how numbers would be written in a specific numeral system.

Computing

(Grades 1–4) Use articles from "Making Numbers Count," such as "Patterns in Addition," "You Can Add," and "You Can Subtract," to extend your teaching of addition and subtraction. For children who enjoy challenges, use number puzzles such as "Backward Puzzles" and "The Minus Mystery."

Chance

(Grades 1–2) Read the article "Sharing Birthdays" on pages 136–137 to children. Have children write their names and birthdates (month and day) on slips of paper and compare them to see if any two birthdates are the same.

(Grades 2–4) Invite children to test their chances using the two boxes described in "Ali Kwazoor's Choice" on pages 138–141 and the activity on pages 142–143. Have two children keep score, and let the group take turns picking a stone from each of the two boxes. Total the number for each box to see which box gave them a better chance to pick a black stone.

Science

Awareness of scientific concerns

(Grades 1–2) Teach poems about the weather in Volume 1. You may also want to read the poems about night in Volume 1 to introduce the explanation of day and night in Volume 6.

Experimenting, observing

(Grades 1–4) Have younger children do selected activities in Volume 6 with your guidance. Let older children work in small groups. Help younger children record their findings on the chalkboard or an experience chart. Older students can record their own findings on a chart or in notebooks.

Testing hypotheses

(Grades 2–4) Read the articles about early explanations of the stars and planets in "Studying the Universe" in Volume 7. Have children listen for ideas about the sun, moon, and planets that people today would not agree with. Then read additional articles from the chapter, or have children read them independently. Have them name the inventions and experiments that have changed people's earlier ideas.

(Grades 2–4) Read the article "Holmes and the *e*" in Volume 10. Let children form four groups. Have each group make up a simple code and write a short saying in the code. Then have groups exchange messages and try to figure out the codes. When a message has been decoded, let the group tell what it says and how they figured it out.

Many children help cook for their family. This boy in the United States is helping to make strawberry jam.

Families play and explore together in all kinds of ways. Some may visit faraway places. This family is hiking in the mountains in France.

What Families Do Together

Families work, learn, grow, and have fun together—each in its own way. Everywhere in the world, family members love and help one another.

Children in many families care for their younger brothers and sisters. This girl in Turkey is keeping an eye on her little brother.

Many families work together. They grow crops and take care of their homes. These children of Fiji in the South Pacific are helping at harvest time.

Many families **worship** together. These children are taking part in a Shinto (SHIHN-toh) religious **ceremony** in Japan.

In families, people teach and learn from each other. This boy on Africa's Ivory Coast is getting a drum lesson.

20   21

Social Studies

The Family

(Grades 1–4) In Volume 11, read articles about the family. In Volume 12, read selected articles from "Families and Neighbors" and talk with children about the families and activities in the photographs. As a group project, create a bulletin-board display on families using children's own poems, stories, and illustrations.

The Community

(Grades 2–4) Enrich studies of housing, food, transportation, or communication by reading aloud or having children read selections in Volume 12. Have children make collages or give presentations on these themes, using photographs, drawings, music, or plays that illustrate examples from around the world.

Geography

(Grades 2–4) Use Chapter 1 of Volume 13 to develop awareness of oceans and continents. Help children locate them on a world map or globe. As they read other selections, have them find the places they read about. For example, in Volume 14, they could locate countries that celebrate a holiday.

Community helpers

(Grades 1–2) Read articles in Volume 12 about how people in communities get along. Have children plan a project to show how helpers in their own community work together. For example, they could make posters or models of doctors, nurses, police officers, trash collectors, and other workers and explain their jobs.

Creative Arts

Music

(Grades 1–2) Have children make the rhythm and wind instruments shown in Volume 3. Let them use the instruments to accompany singing or to play melodies and rhythms that they make up.

Sculpture

(Grades 1–4) Let children try out basic clay techniques in Volume 3 and create real or fanciful animals. Then let them try the activity that uses "found" household objects to make decorative sculptures called assemblages. Older children will enjoy making the owl piñata for a special occasion.

Painting

(Grades 1–2) Use the color-mixing activity in Volume 3 to help children learn primary and secondary colors. Have them use the colors to paint with brushes, or let them try out the string-painting activity to experiment with designs.

(Grades 2–4) Have children make the potstone paint described in Volume 3 and use it to paint posters or a wall mural for a science or social studies project.

Theater

(Grades 2–4) Let children form groups and choose stories from Volume 2. Then have them dramatize it either by taking parts themselves or by making glove puppets or shadow puppets following the Try This! activities from "Theater Around the World" in Volume 3.

(Grades 1–4) Let children act out the African folk tale from "Theater" in Volume 3, using simple props. Costumes for younger children can be simplified by making only the paper-bag masks described in the Try This! activity that follows the play.

Leopard, Goat, and Yam Costumes

Use paper bags for the head gear of other characters' costumes. Make the body costume the same way you made the Sadiki costume, only colored differently.

You Will Need:
large paper bags
scissors
markers
glue
yarn
cardboard
cotton balls
a small stool
a long box
a broom
tape
face paint

To Make a Leopard:
1. Cut a large hole in a bag for the actor's face.

2. Dot the bag with black or brown spots as shown.

3. Draw whiskers and a nose on your face. Glue cardboard ears to the bag.

To Make a Goat:
1. Cut a large hole in a bag for the actor's face.

2. Glue cardboard ears and a goatee, or little beard, to the bag.

3. Cover the rest of the bag with cotton balls. Allow the glue to dry before using the costume.

To Make a Yam:
1. Cut a large hole in a bag for the actor's face.

2. Color the bag orange.

3. Tape leaves made of cardboard to the top.

When you look for props, use your imagination. A long, flat box can be a canoe, and a broom can be an oar. A small stool in a large paper bag would make an excellent boulder. Color the bag gray and crumple it a little.

160   161

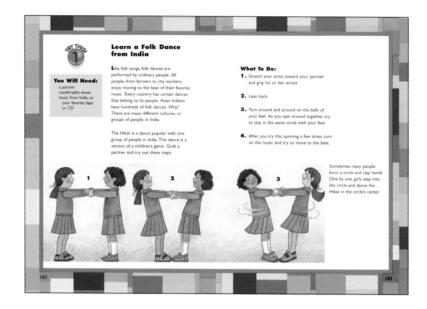

Self-Understanding, Health, and Safety

Games
(Grades 1–4) *Childcraft* contains a variety of games and exercises that provide whole-body movement. Let children try the folk dance of India from "Theater" in Volume 3 and the tag and running games from "What Games Do We Play?" in Volume 12.

Behavior, Manners, and Attitudes
(Grades 1–4) Read and talk about selected articles from "How Do We All Get Along" in Volume 12. Encourage children to develop projects from their discussions, such as making posters about school rules, performing skits about good and bad manners, and creating a bulletin board or notebook of stories and pictures about how people in their families help out at home.

Understanding the Body
(Grades 2–4) Encourage children to use Volume 11 as a reference book to help them understand how their bodies function and grow.

Careers

(Grades 1–2) Have children look through Volume 12 for photographs and illustrations of people at work. Have them tell which ones are like the kinds of work people do in their community. Invite a member of the community who provides a service, such as a police officer, nurse, firefighter, cook, or a supermarket manager, to talk to the class. Or, arrange a short trip to a store, bakery, fire station, library, or other location to see where people work and what they do.

(Grades 1–4) Read "People Who Work with Animals" in Volume 4 and let children talk about the kinds of work that interest them. Invite a worker in your community, such as a veterinarian, veterinary technician, animal shelter worker, or ranger, to speak to the children. Work with the children as one group or smaller groups to write a letter of invitation and to think of questions to ask. Check with the person you plan to invite ahead of time to be sure he or she is willing and is available for a group visit.

(Grades 2–4) Read to children, or have children read, some of the articles that introduce people who work in different areas, such as "People Who Work with Animals" in Volume 4, "Taking Care of Forests" in Volume 5, and "Keeping Track" in Volume 6. Have children look through *Childcraft* for other kinds of jobs that interest them and collect magazine and newspaper pictures, articles, and material from the school library or the Internet about the career topics they choose.

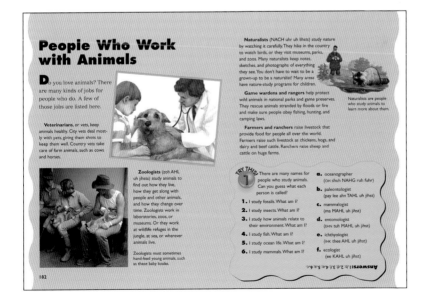

Growth and Development

The preschool years, from about age 3 to 5, are truly formative years, marked by intellectual growth, rapidly developing motor skills, increasing social maturity, and emotional richness. Preschoolers are eager to learn and excited about the world. Children between 5 and 8 years old are alert, high-spirited, and full of ideas and questions. Their first years in school are some of the most crucial years of their education, a time when a solid foundation for learning and positive self-esteem are formed. Parents and teachers play an essential role during these years—guiding, reassuring, teaching, and loving children so that they get the best possible start in their lives.

Preschool Children: 3 to 5 years

The way children use tricycles says a lot about how their motor skills are developing. At 3, they almost surely enjoy riding on trikes. At first, they may be content to sit on the seat. Then they start to use the pedals but don't quite get the hang of them. Sometimes they want to move forward, but the trike goes backward. When they master the basics, they ride along deliberately for a while, proud of their new skills. Soon they discover how far they can go. They don't slow down for turns. They ride as close to people as they can. If they have to stop, they wait until the last second and then come to a fast, hard stop.

Parents also see progress in motor development as preschoolers acquire skill in dressing. By the time they are 3, children can unbutton their clothes, but they have a hard time buttoning them. They cannot tell the back from the front, so they often put pants on backward. They may still need help in putting on shirts, sweaters, and other clothing. When they are 4, preschoolers can dress with little help, although the process may seem to take forever.

The Preschoolers' Development

Social development

The way two preschoolers play together on their tricycles shows changes in social growth as well as motor development. Three-year-olds may simply like to be near each other on their trikes. They may bump each other experimentally. A bit of giggling often goes along with the bumps, but there is seldom much conversation. One child may decide to head off somewhere nearby—at this age, children do not yet go far afield. Another child will probably follow, but not always right away. The social response is not yet quick, sure, and certain.

As they near their fifth birthdays, children are very different. There is almost no sitting still. They are sure to be on the go. Now the children play together. They have plans and they talk about them, sometimes with a few spats. Once they cook up an idea, each one is likely to carry it out with modifications that make the plan his or her own. They have grown into social creatures who get thrills from being with each other.

The pleasure of each other's company and the excitement of doing things together sometimes become so overwhelming that toilet-trained children forget to use the toilet. In their own list of priorities, these preschoolers have put first things first. To them, playing with a friend is more important.

Language development

Another major advance of preschool years, along with social development, is the development of language. By the time children are about 4, they can be chatterboxes.

Preschoolers do not simply chatter, however. Their language involves all the parts of speech, longer sentences, and greater clarity. Language development and social development aid one another. Most preschool children still fight at times. However, they gradually learn to settle disputes with words.

This tremendous growth in speech can be exasperating to adults. Preschoolers seem to talk too much. They frequently interrupt because what they have to say is the most important thing in the world to them. They often talk too loudly. Around age 4, it is common for them to go on a spree of name-calling and experimenting with non-sensical singsongs.

One other characteristic of preschoolers is their never-ending questions. Inquiries increase and become more complex from about 3 years on. "How?" and "Why?" questions continue as children try to understand relationships, how things work, and what they are for.

Preschoolers' Education

Preschoolers' constant questions reflect another side of their development in these years—their intense curiosity and thirst for knowledge. One of the most outstanding characteristics of preschoolers is that they are so completely ready to learn about the world around them, about themselves as a part of that world, about other children, and about adults. Preschoolers are curious, open, and responsive. Their eyes go out to all that is around them. Their hands are tools for exploration.

One of the most important tasks for parents is to keep this burning curiosity and charmed sense of wonder alive. Most parents appreciate curiosity. Sometimes, however, they unintentionally discourage it. Children's curiosity may sometimes be troubling and frightening. Parents worry about safety, so they sometimes curtail children's activities to keep them safe. However, when parents' irritations or worries mount, children may hear "No," "Don't," "Be careful," and "Watch out" too often. Parents must take precautions, of course. But at the same time, they need to avoid giving the message that the world is a bad or dangerous place.

By stimulating children's curiosity, parents help them reach their creative potential. Most important, by nurturing children's curiosity, parents help set them on course for a richer, more fulfilling life.

Taking day trips

Day trips are one of the best ways to bring stimulating experiences to young children. Preschoolers are basically uninformed—they simply

A trip to the store is an adventure.

do not know much yet because they have not experienced much. No one can tell children at this age about the world. They have to see and experience things firsthand, so day trips are perfect learning opportunities.

Day trips for preschoolers should be short. Young children tire easily, and tired, irritable children learn very little. The destination does not have to be spectacular. To young children, the supermarket, post office, park, and other everyday locations are a treat.

A good day trip is one that has a slow, relaxed pace with time for talking. There also ought to be time for several short stops along the way. And on any journey, preschoolers need time to stand and watch, to touch, and to explore. Preschoolers cannot take in all they want to know at a glance. On trips, there are countless opportunities to point out sights children might otherwise miss. In addition, there are many opportunities for children to ask questions that might not otherwise occur to them.

Reading stories out loud gives children a chance to ask questions and learn.

Reading stories

Good storybooks, like good trips, stimulate children. Stories bring a part of the world closer to them so that they can take a closer look at it and come to understand it more fully. Stories may be make-believe or about real people or events. They may involve animals that seem almost human. They may include more adventure than most people have in their everyday lives. But fiction or nonfiction, children's books help preschoolers learn more about the people, events, and objects in their environment.

The trick in reading stories to children is the same as the key to taking successful day trips. Take your time. Do not rush to the end of the story. Let children interrupt to ask questions. Story time should

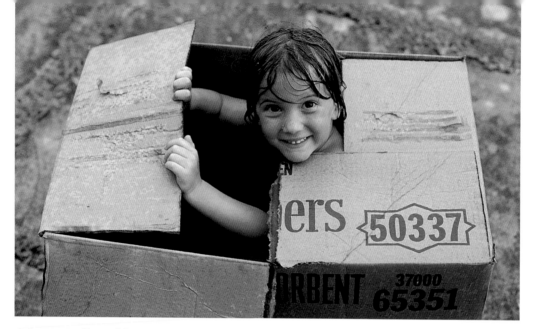

A large cardboard box—one that the child can't close completely—can stimulate highly imaginative play.

be a daily event—a time for companionship and conversation.

Enriching preschoolers' play

To adults looking on, preschoolers seem to spend all of their time just playing. The play of preschool children is far from a waste of time, however. It is a highly significant activity that teaches important emotional, intellectual, and social lessons.

Children at play draw on what they know. They often play house, for example, mostly because life at home is what they know best. The play is imaginative, but it is firmly grounded in reality. The more children know—the more places they have been, the more things they have seen—the richer their play will be. Preschoolers also need toys and other materials with which to carry out their play. The same toys should

be for all to use. Girls may want to play with trains, and boys may want to play house with toy dishes. Nothing should be specifically earmarked for boys or for girls.

Good preschool toys set up rough outlines and give children's fertile minds freedom to fill in the details. A tricycle, for example, is obviously some kind of moving vehicle, but children decide whether it is a horse, ambulance, or rocket. Among the best playthings are boards, boxes, blankets, sand, cartons, wagons, chairs, dolls, simple cars and boats, and other materials that can be used in various ways.

Growing language and social development, increased knowledge, longer attention span, and vastly improved physical coordination all combine to produce the most distinctive characteristic of preschool children: their capacity for make-believe. Children can take on any role that suits their fancy. They can be cowboys, princesses, or tigers. A chair can become a horse, plane, or animal cage.

One kind of imaginative activity special to this age is playing with an imaginary playmate. Imaginary playmates may be someone to boss around or someone who gives support and comfort. These unseen friends can be important to some children. If children begin mentioning some unseen friend, adults should play along. This will give children confidence in the real friends they have in the adults around them.

Television viewing and preschoolers

The fascination television holds for preschoolers is an indication of their thirst for stimulation. TV's fast-moving pictures and continuous sound lure many young children into watching contentedly for hours. For better or for worse, television is a teacher. Television viewing affects children's language and their awareness of the world around them.

Television also provides relaxation and entertainment. However, TV viewing can present hazards. There is reason to worry about the impact of TV's violence on the feelings and morals of children, about the impact of commercials on their taste, and about the effect of long hours of passive watching on their personalities. Parents also must be concerned

because too much TV viewing can rob a family of time for talk and shared activities, and also can deprive children of creative play with friends. These hazards increase if the TV is allowed to become a baby sitter.

Some families react to these concerns by having no TV set. However, when TV is available, it is important for parents to make thoughtful decisions about what programs their children may watch and how long they may watch. Involving preschoolers in these decisions offers them learning experiences about choices and responsibilities.

It also is wise for parents to watch television with their children often enough to discuss with them the ideas, feelings, and values the programs generate. If good programs are available, and if viewing hours are wisely regulated, television can

Preschoolers happily watch TV. They need help in choosing and setting limits.

53

be a positive educational force. For additional information, see "Children, Television, and the Internet" on page 94.

Sending preschoolers to school

Many 3- and 4-year-olds go to preschool. Some are in preschool because their parents want to supplement the stimulation and companionship they can offer at home. Others are in preschool because one or both parents work, and the children need day care. See the article "Choosing Day Care" on page 91.

There are different types of preschools. Some are parent-cooperative schools, which are owned and operated by parents. The parents hire a teacher and take turns helping out in the classroom and doing the other work of the school. Some preschools are operated by community or church groups. Others are run by individuals, corporations, or public-school systems.

At preschool, children move about the room a lot. They begin to learn to live, work, and play together. They learn to take turns, settle disputes fairly, and cooperate. They hear stories and music. They may take short educational trips. They also have the opportunity to express themselves through playthings and artwork. A good preschool has both indoor and outdoor facilities and gives ample time for climbing, balancing, swinging, and other activities that build muscle coordination. Preschool children are almost constantly involved in make-believe play, which gives them the chance to use their initiative, think, plan, develop their attention spans, and build their capacity for problem solving.

Through all these activities, preschools aim to develop in children the habits, attitudes, and skills that will help them in school. Preschools also help children develop their intellectual and physical skills. Preschools aid in the development of good health and safety habits and encourage independence.

Preschool is not for everyone, however. Some children have trouble adjusting to preschool, especially if they've never spent much time away from their parents. Preschool also may be too demanding and stressful for some children. Another downside to preschools is that they can expose children to more viruses, resulting in more illness.

Common Concerns

The preschool period can be a happy time in family life, free from overwhelming problems. One reason is that preschool children can do so much more for themselves. They can be independent in feeding themselves, dressing, and using the toilet. They no longer place the constant physical demands on their parents that they did as infants. Another reason is that preschoolers delight in the world and in the people around them. Their eagerness, openness, and good feelings about being alive can be quite contagious. No age, however, is completely angelic. There are always some rough spots.

Dealing with dawdling

The conflict between young children's time schedules and that of their parents is often a trouble area. Most adults watch the time. They are going somewhere and know exactly how many minutes they need to get there. Young children often stop and watch the world go by. Adults call this action "dawdling." For children, of course, this is simply the way they act. It is a part of the newness of being able to do things for one's self.

The best approach for coping with dawdling is to make some minor adjustments. For example, with eating and dressing, parents should allow as much time as possible so that children can move at their own pace. But if something pressing lies ahead, parents should pitch in with a helping hand to speed up the eating or dressing process. They should not nag or pester. Angry words seldom produce a speed-up. There will be times when reality demands that the meal be ended—for example, when the available time has simply run out. There is no great harm in children experiencing this. In fact, they begin to learn that time has limits. The harm comes only when, as the food is taken away, adult anger, nagging, and complaining come to take its place.

Understanding fears

Some problems arise, too, because it is so easy to forget that 3-year-olds in particular, but also 4-year-olds, are still little, dependent children. When parents forget this, they often are harsher than they should be. This is especially true when these children get frightened. And a wide, unpredictable range of events and sounds and sights can scare them.

The quick, easy response to children's fear is the pep talk: "You're not afraid of a little thing like that, are you?" Preschoolers' only reply, which is often screamed with the whole body, is to say in effect, "I certainly am afraid . . . that's what this fuss is all about." Worse than the pep talk is unsympathetic scoffing and shaming: "Don't be a little baby . . . . Don't be a scaredy cat." When children are afraid of dogs, thunder, or the dark, it hardly helps to have the added fear of losing their parents' love and respect.

An effective first step in dealing with fright is to accept it. Parents should give support and comfort so that frightened children feel strong enough to face the frightening event. Parents can acknowledge fear in supportive ways, such as saying, "All that noise does seem a little scary," while reassuring them that they are not in danger. Sometimes just moving over to be close is all the support that is needed. Children who are deeply upset have to be held, patted, and comforted. The goal is to give enough support so that they feel better, without protecting them so much that they feel pushed back into babyhood. When frightened children have calmed down a bit, parents can try to teach them how to cope with the experience the next time it happens. The more competence children have, the fewer fears there will be.

The most upsetting fear of all occurs when children think their parents do not love them. Any one of a wide variety of events can start this unhappy train of thought. Separation is a problem. When young children are left alone in a strange new setting such as a hospital, a doctor's office, or preschool, they can easily translate "Separation—they are leaving me" into "Separation—they don't love me." Harshness, coldness, and busyness can have the same effect. Children in these situations can feel alone and unprotected.

Sometimes events that parents think ought to make children feel grown-up have the opposite effect, and children become fearful. Getting accustomed to a new baby in the family and starting school are two events that parents often think will make children feel more mature but often stimulate fear instead. In such situations, it is best for parents to be understanding until children are able to adjust to the new situation and overcome any fears.

Developing discipline

Developing good discipline in children is one of the most important jobs of parenthood. But this vital task takes time, patience, and understanding.

Many parents believe that children resent discipline. These parents not only hesitate to punish their children but also seldom use effective ways of building discipline. They want to be good to their children and end up being too lenient. Undisciplined children never know the limits of acceptable behavior, and this is very unsettling for them. They need someone to teach them what is right or wrong, and why.

Getting a child's attention is a first step in explaining the rules and teaching appropriate behavior.

Wise parents do not shrink from disciplining their children. They try to figure out why their children misbehave and then take whatever action best fits the situation. For example, young children often misbehave because they simply do not know any better. When this is the problem, one appropriate method of discipline is to patiently explain what the rules are and why rules are important. The goal is to teach so that children will understand.

Teaching as a method of discipline is effective only if parents believe in what they are saying,

however. They must convey to children that the lesson is important. They must take time to make sure that the child is paying attention and not simply listening with only half an ear. When a parent says, "Stop," and explains why, the child's action must stop—at least for that moment.

Reasoning is an effective but slow method of discipline. It is slow because children cannot be expected to learn after discussing an incident just once. They must hear the lesson over and over again. But in the long run, reasoning is a good method because it helps children learn values that they can use as they grow and mature. It is also a method that respects children's growing independence.

Besides teaching and reasoning, using praise is one of the best ways to encourage good behavior, especially when it directly follows good behavior. For example, if children come to the table with clean hands, or act in a way that is expected, immediate praise should be offered. Welcome approval reinforces children's good behavior, making it more likely to be repeated.

"Not knowing any better" is only one reason for misbehavior. At times, children do the wrong thing because of what is going on around them. When this seems to be the case, the way to discipline is not through discussion but through action. Parents should change the setting to make it easier for children to be good. This approach is especially useful with children too young to understand words, but it also works with older children. For example, things that toddlers should not touch should be put out of reach. Older children who have to sit for a long time will behave much better if they are given a book to read or a game to play.

Some misbehavior is rooted in children's feelings. Children have to feel right to act right. Some children are driven to misbehavior because they desperately need more love, more attention, or a feeling of importance. They do things they know they should not do. A jealous child, for example, may hurt a baby sister or brother. The temptation is to punish children driven by upset feelings, but the surest way to help them is to give them the love or attention or importance their behavior shows they need.

Parents have to be thoughtful in choosing an approach to discipline. They need to pick the one that fits each child and each situation. This sensitive process of deciding what action to take itself contributes to discipline. It is an expression of love, and the foundation of all good behavior is children's sense of being loved. Children unconsciously identify with parents who show their love. Slowly but steadily, they will take on the attitudes and values of their parents. What is learned through this process of identification does not reveal itself immediately, but the lessons are instilled in children. Good behavior will evolve in time.

The Health and Safety of Preschoolers

For information on growth, see "Following the Growth of Young Children" on page 85.

Dental care

Regular dental examinations are the surest way for children to enjoy healthy teeth that will last a lifetime. Children's first visit to the dentist should be made at the age of 3, soon after all the primary teeth are in. Before their first visit, children should accompany a parent on a routine dental visit. Most dentists will allow children to sit in the dentist's chair, examine some of the instruments, and become acquainted with the dentist and the surroundings. Then the first real visit will not be strange and scary.

At home, parents should encourage children to brush after every meal and snack. Parents should ask the dentist when their children should begin to floss. Parents should allow children to pick out a toothbrush and supply an attractive cup for rinsing the mouth to make brushing more fun.

Good dental care begins with good brushing habits in preschool years.

Avoiding accidents

Preschoolers are accident-prone. In fact, hundreds of children under 4 years old die every month because of serious accidents, most of which can be prevented.

Accidents often happen because parents are not aware of what their children can do. By the time they are preschoolers, children can walk, run, climb, jump, and explore everything. Because of all the new things they can do, this stage can be a very dangerous time. It is the parents' responsibility to protect children from injury. Children have a hard time remembering "No" while exploring. In addition, they don't completely understand danger.

Parents should teach children how to recognize and react to dangerous situations and how to develop sound safety habits. In addition, parents should be good role models of safety habits, make rules and enforce them, create a safe environment, and be aware that preschoolers need constant supervision.

Here are some suggestions for teaching safety to preschoolers:

- As situations arise, teach preschoolers rules about street and traffic safety, "stranger danger," animal safety, water safety, fire safety, and playground safety. For help, parents can talk to their child's pediatrician and refer to books from bookstores or the library.

- Watch some appropriate television shows with preschoolers. This is an excellent way to teach safety by identifying and discussing hazardous and unrealistic situations with them.

- Read age-appropriate books about safety. These are widely available at bookstores or libraries.

- Take children to safety programs sponsored by community agencies such as the local police department, fire department, or the American Red Cross.

- Make preschoolers active members in "safety surveillance." For example, make children responsible for picking up toys after play and storing them in safe places. Children can tag along on periodic safety checks of the home. This will give them the opportunity to see how smoke alarms work, how the house is made safer for younger siblings, how play areas are checked for safety, and so on. Give children responsibility for reminding others to wear their seat belts in cars and for checking the street for cars before others are allowed to cross.

- Conduct family fire drills. Involve children in the drills and encourage them to ask questions about things they don't understand.

Making the home safe for preschoolers is a never-ending task.

Their growing abilities and curiosity keep safety-conscious parents constantly on their toes. To begin, parents should get down—literally—to their children's level and take a look around the house from their perspective. This exercise alone points out many of the hazards that lurk about the house, such as furniture with sharp corners protruding at their level or strong cleaning materials within easy reach. Here are a few other tips for creating a safe home environment for preschoolers.

- To avoid falls, use gates on stairways and install window guards above the first floor.
- Find something safe for children to do while adults are cooking. If children are underfoot, hot liquids, grease, and hot foods can spill and cause serious burns. If children do get burned, immediately run cold water over the burned area. Then cover the burn loosely with a bandage or clean cloth.
- If a gun is kept in the house, keep it unloaded and in a locked place separate from the ammunition.
- Buy and install smoke and carbon monoxide detectors. Test their batteries every month to be sure they work. Change the batteries twice a year.
- Set the water temperature in the home to no higher than 120 °F. (49 °C).
- Use only household products and medicines that are absolutely necessary, and keep them safely capped and out of sight and reach. Post the phone number of the poison center or doctor near the telephone. Have syrup of ipecac on hand. It is used to induce vomiting in certain kinds of poisoning, but do not use it unless you are told to do so by a poison center or a doctor.
- Lock up or make inaccessible all areas where tools, knives, matches, and other potentially hazardous items are kept.

Above all else, parents' primary responsibility for the safety of preschoolers is supervision—both at home and away. Parents should thoroughly investigate the homes of baby sitters, preschools, and day-care centers. They should choose only those that are safe and have reputable care providers.

Enjoying Your Preschooler

The preschool years can be a delightful time for families. The children are now beyond the age when they need constant physical care, and they have not yet reached the age when they will be so wrapped up in school demands and friends that parents feel squeezed out of their children's lives. Parents are lucky—and obviously the children are lucky—when whole families can find time to enjoy these years together.

These years are a time for companionship—a time for walks together and short trips. They are a time for shared experiences at home. Children have their moments of wanting to work along with parents, helping in their own way with cooking, cleaning, and other interesting household and yard chores.

These years are a time for words, stories, and music. They are a time for reading together and talking about books. They are the years for listening to children and for talking with children. Children ask all about the ins and outs of their environment and give parents ample opportunity for explaining and interpreting the world. Preschoolers' behavior gives parents many opportunities to talk about values and discipline.

These years are a time for the shared awe and delight in the charming, never-ending variety of our world: bugs and nuts and bolts, clamshells and cars, snake skins and leaves, the birth of baby kittens and the screeching of a bright red fire engine.

Parents who work outside the home must make careful plans to find the time to share all this with their children. The special effort it takes proves very rewarding to parents and children alike.

Lucky parents and lucky preschoolers enjoy many times together. But wise parents know that even during these early years, children need more people than just their parents. These are wonderful years for children to come to know their wider family of grandparents, uncles, aunts, and cousins. These are the years when parents can help their children find friends in the family doctor and dentist. They are also a good time for children to discover the librarian in the public library.

Equally important, preschoolers need friends of their own age. Accommodating children's increasingly strong social drive is one of the values of a good childcare center for children whose parents work or who are from one-parent homes. It is also one of the reasons for preschools. Parents also can satisfy their children's need and yearning for companionship

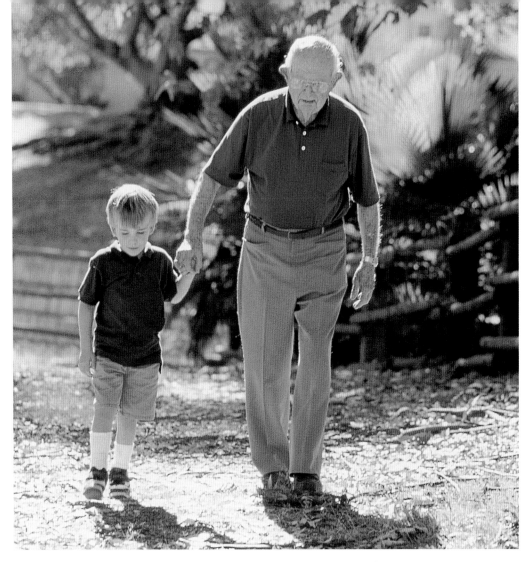

For a preschool child, a grandparent can be a special friend as well as a family member.

through organizing play groups or taking turns with friends and neighbors in watching each other's children. Some parents invite their children's friends to come to the house to play or to join the family on a day trip.

It's easy to overestimate what preschoolers can do and expect too much from them. It also is easy to underestimate them and offer too little physical challenge and social and intellectual stimulation. Parents' best safeguard and guide is to keep a watchful eye, judge from children's behavior how they are feeling at the moment—big and brave and bold, or young and dependent on grown-ups—and enjoy them just the way they are.

School-Age Children: 5 to 8 years

It is easy to see how much 8-year-olds have changed since age 5. It is not so easy to look at 5-year-olds and realize how much they will change in the next 3 years. It is, however, important that parents of children entering school be able to look ahead. Parents should be aware of the many changes that will occur in their children during the early school years so that they will be better able to meet children's physical, mental, emotional, and social needs.

The School-Age Child's Development

Following social development

At this age, boys mostly play with boys and girls with girls. When no children of the same sex live in the neighborhood, children usually find playmates in school or through a religious organization, group lessons, sports, or a group with whom the family socializes.

Children between 5 and 8 years have a lot of initiative. They are interested in accomplishments and want to do things well. They need encouragement and respect.

School gives children new opportunities for social development.

School-age children like the feeling of responsibility—of doing something necessary to make the home operate smoothly. Children should be given some responsibilities as part of the household. Tasks should be those that children are capable of handling, such as making their own beds, cleaning their rooms, feeding family pets, setting the table, or putting groceries away.

When children start school, an important person enters their lives—their teacher. The teacher is often the first adult friend that children make on their own. Most children are aware of every detail of their teacher's appearance and respond to every smile or frown. If they like their teacher, they want their parents to feel the same way.

Using parents as role models

Children model themselves largely on their parents. They do so mainly by identifying with a parent. The things parents do and say—and the way they do and say them—will strongly influence children's behavior. This is why it is important for parents to behave like the type of person they want their children to become.

Parents' actions also affect the self-image that children form through identification. Children who see mainly positive qualities in their parents will likely learn to see themselves in a positive way. Children who observe chiefly negative qualities in their parents will have difficulty seeing positive qualities in themselves. Children may modify their self-image, however, as they become increasingly influenced by peer group standards in later years.

Isolated events, even dramatic ones, do not necessarily have a permanent effect on children's behavior. Children interpret such events according to how their parents deal with them, their own established attitudes, and their previous training. For example, children who know they are loved can accept the divorce of their parents or a parent's early death. On the other hand, if children feel unloved, they may interpret such events as a sign of rejection or punishment.

In the same way, children are not equally influenced by toys, books, magazines, television programs, and Internet activities. The effect of an activity or experience depends on how children interpret it. Children's interpretations, in turn, depend on their standards of behavior. For instance, violent behavior on television may heighten the aggressive tendencies of children who consider such behavior permissible. However, children who have learned that violent behavior is wrong are less likely to be influenced by TV violence. The day-to-day behavior and lessons of parents have a more powerful influence on children than do isolated events and experiences.

Making visits away from home

Through visits away from home, school-age children gradually develop social graces and independence. They try out new foods and become accustomed to unfamiliar routines. They learn new skills by sharing family chores in other households. They make friends with children in other communities. Children also develop skills in relating to people away from home. They learn that all families are not alike. Visits to homes of friends for playing, eating a meal, or spending the night all add to their social development.

Before allowing a visit away from home, parents should consider a number of things. For example, does the child really want to spend the night away from home? Is the host family reasonable and flexible? Will they be patient as the child tries to fit into their situation? Have they been told of the child's special needs? Is the child a bed-wetter—a condition that would be acceptable in some households and unacceptable in others? Does the child have occasional nightmares? Is the child allergic to certain foods or materials? Prospective hosts should be told about any special needs of the child before final plans for the visit are made. This gives them

Preschool children can help parents pick out new clothes.

the chance to reconsider if the child's needs seem too great a responsibility for them.

Making choices

During the school-age years, children learn to make choices. And parents can find many ways to give children the opportunity to make them. For example, children may have definite preferences in food and the way food is prepared and served. Some children eat vegetables only if they are raw. Some prefer fruit juice to fresh fruit. So long as the alternatives are convenient and children are eating nutritionally balanced meals, parents should allow children to make food choices. The experience adds to their personal development.

Clothing presents still more opportunities for children to make choices. Parents can allow children to decide what to wear each day.

Children also can help pick out new clothes at the store. At this age, children may start to be caught up in fads. Sometimes, gym shoes are the important symbol, and the brand name or label may be as important as the style. Hairstyle, jewelry, the cut of pants, the type of jacket—all of these things may be driven by popular trends. Again, parents should respect children's choices with regard to their appearance, within reason.

Receiving an allowance

Giving a regular allowance can be a worthwhile educational experience for children. An allowance gives children a realistic, firsthand experience in planning how to spend or save money and how to get full value for it. An allowance also provides children with a natural opportunity to learn arithmetic and to begin to develop a sense of logic.

Children may buy unwisely at first or spend all their money immediately, forgetting that no more will be forthcoming for several days. However, this may help children to learn to choose wisely and spend carefully, because an allowance also involves making choices.

Parents may wish to start with a small weekly allowance and give the same sum on the same day of each week. As children learn the possibilities and limitations of the allowance, and as their needs multiply, the amount can be increased. Children will become ready to take on the additional responsibility of managing the money needed for school expenses—bus fare, school supplies, or lunch money. As the amount of allowance grows, parents may want to discuss how to budget the allowance. They can help children figure out how much must be spent each week on essential expenses. Parents also may want to talk about ways of spending or saving any extra money—such as money that they earn doing special chores or receive as gifts.

An allowance should be considered a child's share of the family income and, therefore, should be no more than the family can afford. An allowance should also be considered a child's own money. Parents should allow children to make mistakes and learn from them. Allowances should not be withheld because of disobedience, poor grades, or unwise spending. An allowance should not be considered a bargaining tool to guarantee children's good behavior, nor should it be considered a bribe.

Following motor development

"Slow but steady" characterizes the development of motor skills during the school-age years. For example, many 5-year-olds have not yet mastered writing. The small muscles that control fingers and hands are still developing. Writing also requires hand-eye coordination, which also is not yet well developed in some 5-year-olds. Even 6-year-olds still find writing difficult.

Seven-year-olds usually concentrate hard when writing. They grip the pencil tightly and usually hold it close to the point. Their letters are uneven in size. By the time they are 8, their hand-eye coordination and the small muscles in their hands and fingers are much better developed, and they write more evenly and easily. Physical maturity and better concentration also aid children's writing.

Children's large muscles also are still developing. Girls at this age are better coordinated than boys. Both boys and girls are physically active—they run climb, skip, hop, and jump, and they like to be on the go at all times. Too long a time assigned to a chair and desk without a break can lead to restlessness and boredom.

Blocks, paints, and other art activities involve both large-muscle and small-muscle motor skills.

Following other physical characteristics

Growth in height and weight from age 5 to 8 is also slow but steady. The average child adds 2 to 2.4 inches (5 to 6 centimeters) in height and 5 or 6 pounds (2 or 3 kilograms) in weight each year. For more information, see "Following the Growth of Young Children" on page 85.

A distinguishing characteristic of school-age children is their smile—and the wide-open spaces that show where primary teeth have fallen out to make room for permanent teeth. Six-year molars are breaking through, and permanent incisors are beginning to appear.

The Early School Years

Starting school

Starting school is a major adventure and a dramatic change for most children. Most of them can hardly wait to start school. They take this challenge in stride because their normal growth—in language, attention span, social interests, curiosity, and independence—enables them to welcome school without strain. There are, however, a few ways parents can make it even easier for children to begin their school life without emotional upsets.

Adjusting to school will be easier if children have had the experience of being away from home without their parents. Children who have often gone to the store with a neighbor, eaten lunch at a friend's house, or visited nearby relatives—or who have attended preschool or daycare—usually have no problems with leaving home and adjusting to the classroom environment.

School adjustment also will be easier for children who have experienced accepting people other than their parents as authorities. Children who have been in the care of good baby sitters, for example, will probably have less trouble accepting a teacher. Children who have played with their friends in a neighborhood backyard or a house down the street, responding to whatever adult was in charge of the play, have a good foundation for working with a teacher.

Most children beginning kindergarten or first grade know other children who will be their classmates. Seeing familiar faces helps children adjust. If children have no friends in school, parents can invite one or two future classmates over to play or for lunch so that there will indeed be one or two familiar faces on the first day of school.

Most schools set aside a day for children to visit their prospective classroom for a short time and meet some of their future classmates. A

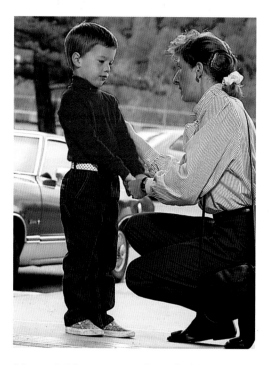

Many children are ready and able to leave home and adjust to school.

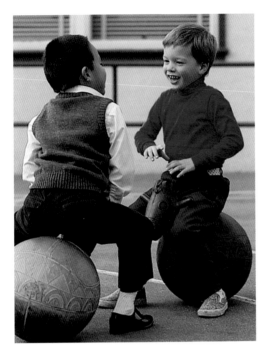

Seeing familiar faces and finding new friends make the first days of school exciting.

language arts, social sciences, mathematics, science, music, and art. Sometimes these subjects are not taught as separate courses. Instead, they may be integrated into a total experience.

Children learn best through first-hand experiences—seeing, hearing, touching, smelling, and above all, doing. Children need these first-hand experiences before they can learn to read. Some children arrive at school able to print, identify letters, or even read a little. Others are unable to do these things. Both are perfectly normal. By the end of first grade, most children have learned to associate the sounds in words with written letters, and they are able to spell many words by

few typical activities may be carried out to let children sample what a school day will be like.

Building a foundation for learning

Some school-age children approach learning in a systematic manner. They proceed in logical, methodical ways. Others are cautious. They move forward only when they are sure of themselves. Still others dive in and then look around. Both parents and teachers must understand and accommodate each child's unique way of learning.

In the early grades, children are taught to read, write, and work with numbers. The curriculum includes

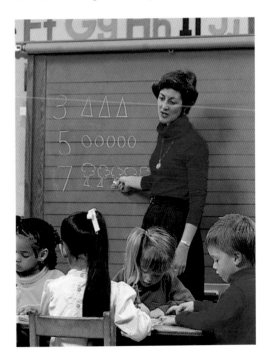

Reading, writing, and numbers are basic learning tools.

applying simple phonetic rules. Many are reading.

Social studies in these early years generally include learning about people and the world around them. A group of kindergartners may study their town and the neighborhoods and people who make it work. Children are encouraged to discuss their observations and ask questions. What begins as a study of "our community" in the early school years grows into the study of geography, economics, consumer education, ecology, science, safety, history, mapmaking, and map reading in the years to come.

Science is experienced firsthand, too. For example, children may prove that a magnet will only attract things made of iron by conducting experiments with a magnet and various objects. Then children may make magnets. Next, they may make a compass or a buzzer to discover how magnets are used in different objects. By making these items, children begin to understand how they work.

School-age children enjoy music and art. Most of them love to sing, and some even make up their own songs. They use such rhythm instruments as drums, cymbals, and tambourines. They like moving, dancing, and dramatizing or marching to music. Most school-age children like to paint, work with clay, and draw pictures with crayons and pencils.

School-age children also like stories and poetry. They enjoy being read to, an activity that not only stimulates imagination and improves concentration, but also helps strengthen the bond between the teacher and children. When given the opportunity, children compose delightful stories and often write interesting poems.

The monthly calendar is also a learning device. At first, the calendar does not mean much to children. But as days go by, they begin to learn the days of the week, dates in sequence, weekdays and weekend days, and the meaning of time and its components. Children have experiences with words, letters, numbers, holidays, and seasons.

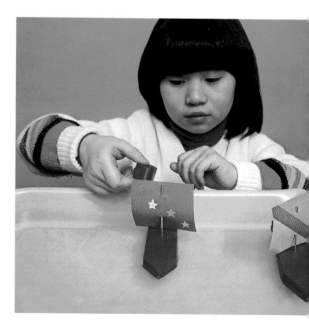

Magnets provide fascinating science experiences for young children.

Conferences give parents and teachers a chance to raise questions, exchange observations, and set goals.

Establishing the home-school relationship

The basis for the home-school relationship forms during the early years of school. Parents should try to meet children's teachers before school starts. At this meeting, parents should talk openly about their children. Then, when school starts, the teacher will already know something about the children and will be able to help each one develop.

Most schools provide time for parent-teacher conferences throughout the school year. Parent-teacher conferences serve both teachers and parents by helping them to identify and discuss the unique needs and interests of each child.

At conferences, teachers can describe their goals for the year, give parents samples of their children's work, and discuss children's behavior, habits, attitudes, capabilities, strengths, and weaknesses. Conferences give parents a chance to raise questions that cannot be answered adequately by report cards, and they give teachers an opportunity to learn more about the children's lives outside of school. Conferences help parents and teachers work together to help children reach their potential. Parents also may want to meet the parents of other children in the classroom. This will help them better understand friendships and the dynamics of the classroom.

Health and Safety of Young School-Age Children

It is important that children have a physical examination before entering school. In fact, many school systems require it and will not allow children to attend school without a tuberculin skin test and immunizations against measles, mumps, rubella (German measles), diphtheria, tetanus, pertussis (whooping cough), polio, chicken-pox, and hepatitis B. Eye, ear, and dental examinations also are encouraged at this time. Finding any vision, hearing, or other problems before school begins will help children achieve more at school.

Getting to and from school safely

Getting to school is one of the most important events of the day for school-age children. If children will be walking, they should be taught to walk safely. Here are a few tips:

- Don't allow younger children to cross streets alone.
- Model and teach good pedestrian behavior.
- Teach children to make eye contact with drivers—to make sure drivers see them—before crossing in front of a stopped car.
- Teach children to cross streets at corners, using traffic signals and crosswalks whenever possible.

- Have children look left, right, and left again when crossing a street and teach them to continue looking as they cross.
- Teach children to never run into the street.
- Have children wear reflective materials if walking at dusk and/or dawn.
- Where there are no sidewalks, children should walk facing traffic, as far to the left as possible.

If children this age must walk alone, they should be taught to go directly to and from school without stops or side trips. They also should be told to never accept rides from strangers or even to stop to talk with strangers. These instructions should be given not in a frightening manner but matter-of-factly, so that children learn them just as they learn any other rule. Children also should know their full name and street address before they begin school, in case they get lost.

In some communities, children ride a school bus. Generally, these buses pick children up at designated corners. Here are some school-bus safety tips. If children will be riding the bus, parents should review these tips with them.

- Arrive at the bus stop early. Wait for the bus to come to a complete

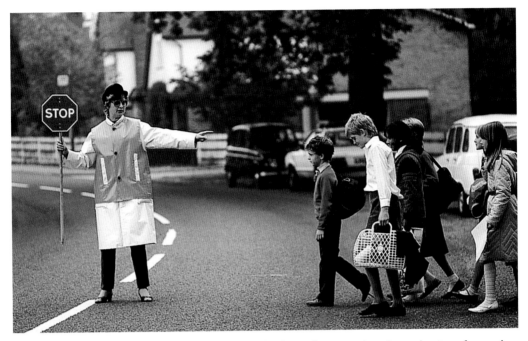

Whether children walk to school or ride the bus, they need to learn basic safety rules.

stop before approaching the street. Watch for cars, and avoid the bus driver's blind spot.

- Stay seated on the bus at all times and keep the head and arms inside the bus while riding.
- When getting off the bus, wait until the bus comes to a complete stop. Exit from the front, using the handrail to avoid falls.
- Remind children to cross the street at least 10 feet in front of a school bus. Children should wait for adults on the same side of the street as the school bus loading and unloading zone.

In addition, parents can check to see that someone on the bus is responsible for helping younger children board and exit. They should also check whether the bus is in good condition, whether the driver is reputable and qualified, and whether the roads traveled are safe. If in doubt, parents should contact a school official.

Dealing with common illnesses

Communicable diseases are quite common during the school-age years. Some can be avoided by vaccination, but parents of school-age children must learn to take in stride the usual run of colds, sore throats, and coughs.

If children have been exposed to a communicable disease such as measles or chickenpox, a teacher or school nurse will probably send a note home informing parents of the fact and explaining what symptoms to look for. If children develop the symptoms, they should be kept home from school and seen by a doctor, if necessary.

Another common health problem in schools is head lice. Lice are tiny insects that infest the body. Head lice infestations have nothing to do with cleanliness. Lice spread from person to person easily, and anyone can get them. They adhere to hair and fibers and lay their eggs near hair shafts. The larvae that hatch, called nits, may look like dandruff. Lice produce substances that irritate the skin and scalp and can cause severe itching.

If a child at school has head lice, a note will go home to the parents of all children in the classroom, telling how to check for and treat lice. All children who have come in contact with someone who has head lice should be examined. Head lice are most commonly found on the scalp behind the ears and near the neckline at the back of the neck. The symptoms of infestation include a tickling feeling of something moving in the hair, itching caused by an allergic reaction to the bites, irritability, and sores on the head caused by scratching. If parents are unsure whether children have head lice, the child should be checked by a doctor or the school nurse.

Common Concerns

Unless children have been in a day-care setting or preschool, the early school years present a new social environment and challenges unlike any they have ever had before. At home, it was taken for granted that they belonged and were accepted. This gave them a natural security. Certainly at home, they had to adapt to parents and brothers and sisters. However, the home atmosphere is unlike the challenge and interaction provided by contact with 20 to 30 classmates. Because of these new conditions, differences related to sex and age may become apparent, and certain problems may appear in children's lives.

Understanding sex differences

Girls may appear more mature than boys when they start school because they have a more rapid maturation rate than boys do during these years. Physically and emotionally, girls are likely to become organized and ready to work with symbolic and abstract tasks sooner than boys are. However, both boys and girls are ready to learn and to share knowledge.

Differences in the abilities of children in a classroom can be helpful to teachers. Consider the following situation: Patty can print her name correctly when she enters kindergarten, while Terrell, who is the same age, may only recognize the first letter of his name. This does not mean that Patty is the brighter of the two. It may mean merely that someone took the time to teach her what she knows, and she may have been eager to learn this. Terrell, on the other hand, may solve building problems easily in block play or use colors imaginatively. Having classmates who can print their names and a helpful teacher may encourage him to learn. He may also discover that he can use his skills and share his knowledge with other children.

Regarding age differences

No matter how bright children may be, it may make a difference whether they have lived barely five years or almost six years when they enter kindergarten. Being younger than most classmates can place some children at a disadvantage.

Suppose September 1 is the cutoff date for entering kindergarten. Children who became 5 years old on September 2 of the previous school year will be in the same class with children who turn 5 on September 1 of the current year. Children entering kindergarten at nearly six years are likely to be better coordinated, more able to control impulses, and more able to concentrate on a learning task.

Regardless of intellectual ability, some kindergarten children cannot bridge the gap between themselves and their older, more physically mature classmates. They also may have difficulty conforming to the arbitrary learning timetable of many schools. Younger kindergarten children should be observed for the development of social and other school-related readiness skills. If they remain far behind their classmates in acquiring these skills, a developmental evaluation should be considered.

Coping with school problems

School is such an important part of children's lives that all children face some problems in the many years that they spend there. Therefore, parents and teachers must stay in close communication.

Problems that have their origin in school may become apparent only at home. For example, children who operate under tension all day long at school may seem earnest and conscientious to their teachers. Parents may be the only ones to see the outbursts that reflect the strain these children are feeling. Similarly, some children may appear at home to be working smoothly. Teachers, watching these children in a differ-

ent setting and in comparison with other children the same age, may be first to notice that a problem exists. Parents and teachers must have some means of sharing their insights so that problems can be identified and solved before they become too severe.

Dealing with unwillingness to go to school

The first sign of a school problem may be an unwillingness to go to school. Some kindergarten and first-grade children show their fear of school openly. They cry, say that they hate school, and are unwilling to leave home. Sometimes unwillingness to go to school shows in disguised form through frequent complaints of illness or prolonged dawdling and other delaying tactics. A fear or dislike of school can be a troubling problem.

The causes can be many, and they vary from child to child. The only good solution is the one that gets to the root of the difficulty. Some children may be unwilling to go to school because they have not had sufficient experience in being away from home; others because they find the large group setting overwhelming. Still others have fears about their school experience, such as riding alone on the bus or often having to deal with aggressive children on their own. The unwilling-

Some children deal with the demands of the classroom more easily than others.

ness also can be a sign that children are experiencing learning difficulties.

When parents and teachers begin to talk together and pool their information, they usually can uncover the difficulties and make plans that help children identify the problems, cope with them, and possibly solve them. The parents' attitudes are important while this search is going on. On the one hand, they must feel sympathetic to children who have problems. Life can be uncomfortable when something is going wrong. On the other hand, parents must have confidence that problems can be solved, and they must communicate this. When parents assure their children that they stand by them and that they will help them find solutions to their problems, they help build children's self-confidence and security. Of course, children only remain confident and secure when their parents follow through on their assurances to help.

Coping with problems related to success and failure

As children move further in their school careers, more difficulties are likely to stem from their successes and failures in academic work and from relationships with classmates and teachers. Children are like many adults. They cannot go through day after day of failure, not liking their assigned tasks, and not enjoying people with whom they associate, without feeling unhappy. Adults can change jobs when they feel this way. Most children cannot physically leave school. Their only alternative is to leave mentally—to daydream, give up, or rebel.

Again, there is no single answer to every child's trouble. A patient, mutual search by parents and teacher is the only wise procedure. A physical difficulty, with vision or hearing in particular, is sometimes a cause. Schoolwork puts the first great strain on hearing and vision. A complete physical examination is often a wise first step.

Children vary greatly in their ability to do schoolwork. They vary in intelligence, growth rate, and ability to handle specific kinds of subject matter. Possibly, without meaning to, either parents at home or teachers at school may be asking more of children than they are able to do. When expectations are too high, children almost always do not succeed as well as they could. A school's solution is sometimes to readjust its programs, aiming more realistically at goals that children can achieve. Parents sometimes must adjust their expectations at home so that children feel successful and self-assured.

Some children have problems because they are underachievers. They have considerably more ability than they use, and they glide through their days, operating on only a small part it. On the face of it, this may not seem like a problem. However, children are much more content when they work up to their ability. Unchallenged, these children can turn to misbehavior, such as acting out in class or bullying, that reflects their discontent.

It is easier to overlook children who are underachieving than those who are failing. Failing children quickly attract adult attention. Underachievers can slide by unnoticed. Parents and teachers need to talk together so that such problems are not ignored. A parent's account, for example, of a child's unusual persistence and success with a hobby or out-of-school activity may signal that the child has more ability than the school has tapped.

Coping with family problems and school

The demands of schoolwork sometimes uncover tension children are feeling at home. Children who worry about some aspect of their family life have difficulty concentrating and meeting the rigors of academic work. These difficulties may well go unnoticed before school. Once in school, however, many school counselors may spot the problems and look for ways to treat them. Families seeking help with problems may be able to turn to their communities for assistance. Many communities have child guidance centers or service societies that can help with family problems.

Understanding social problems

School is not exclusively academic work. A school is a social center, too. Children's social acceptance or rejection plays a major role in their school life, and it often has repercussions on how well they learn.

Problems in children's social life are perhaps the hardest of all for adults to solve. Adults cannot force children to like one another. They can, however, sometimes help children to be more likable. Teaching children who are "picked on" some skills that other children value is one useful approach. Helping children make friends by inviting classmates home after school is another way. Teachers also can use seating arrangements or school activities to help bring together children who may learn to like each other.

Finding solutions to school problems

As with all problems involving human interaction, children's school problems take time, patience, and wisdom to solve. In some instances, it takes a long time to work out a solution. Some of the factors that can be involved—for example, large class size, a teacher's long-established way of teaching, or a family's way of treating a child—cannot be modified overnight.

Parents and teachers must feel good will and be patient in working together if answers are to be found. It is important to recognize, too, that there are some problems children have to solve for themselves. In these instances, parents, teachers, and school administrators can only assist by helping children acquire the tools to deal with problems.

Enjoying Young School-Age Children

Between the ages of 5 and 8, most children are open, energetic, and easy to get along with. It is a prime time for adults to help set children on a positive course in school. These early school years are formative years in children's lives and can serve as a foundation for good preteen and teenage behavior. Here are some suggestions on how to make the most of children's early school years.

- Tailor expectations to fit children's abilities; then they will be encour-aged to continue learning. If children are expected to meet unrealistic goals, they could become discouraged and disinterested in school.

- Emphasize the positive. Stress the things children can do and do not overemphasize achievement, especially in school. Children should not be told that they have to be the best. Instead, they should be told to try their best.

- Do not give children rewards for good grades. Such rewards make

Assigning simple chores and praising responsible behavior are good ways to help children take on and meet responsibilities.

children believe they must always be compensated for doing well.

- Establish a good relationship with children's teachers. If children can do better work in school, parents should discuss the problem with teachers. Teachers can suggest effective ways to help children succeed in school.

- Continue reading to children. School-age children like stories and enjoy being read to. Reading sessions also help parents build a positive relationship with children, which can help in later years when the lines of communication between parents and children become more difficult. Listening to stories can also help improve children's comprehension and build vocabulary. Children can understand and enjoy language and ideas in books that they cannot yet read on their own.

- Good communication with children requires good listening skills. If children have something to say, parents need to take the time to listen, even if what children have to say seems of little importance.

- Help children develop a sense of responsibility. Assign some chores—drying dishes, taking the garbage out, making the bed, keeping a clean room. Also, recognize and encourage responsible behavior by praise. Remember that responsible behavior also includes such everyday events as getting up and going to school and coming home promptly after school.

- Give children choices in hobbies or weekend activities. Do not force such things as taking dancing or music lessons solely because other children the same age are taking them. Respect the uniqueness and individuality of each child.

- Children need help that allows them to develop their own abilities. Too much help may make them overly dependent. Too little help may result in feelings of inadequacy or frustration. Give children the right kind of help. For example, if a child writes a letter and asks for help in spelling certain words, give help with only those words. Do not rewrite, correct, or criticize the letter.

The most important way to help school-age children be successful is to accept them as they are and inspire them to become what they want to be. And what do most children want? They want to be liked, to have interesting work to do, and to be respected. This is human and universal and highly possible if the home and school work together to achieve this end.

For Special Consideration

At one time or another, parents face special challenges related to family upheavals or to children's health and education needs. This section includes discussions of a number of challenges that parents of young children often face. It also offers ways to help parents deal with these challenges and suggests places to find further assistance.

Following the Growth of Young Children

Physical growth begins with conception. It is influenced by many factors, some of which we are only beginning to understand. The interaction between genetics and environment results in a range of possibilities for children's height.

Assessing growth

After age 2 or 3, children begin to assume their individual growth patterns, and they grow at the rate that they will follow until just before puberty. At age 3, children grow 2.8 to 3.2 inches (7 to 8 centimeters) per year, and between ages 4 and 9, they grow 2 to 2.4 inches (5 to 6 centimeters) per year. Growth rates of less than 2 inches (5 centimeters) per year after age 2 signal the need for medical assessment. Because absolute heights at any given age may vary, it is the pattern of growth that needs to be assessed.

The growth in height and weight for boys and girls at different ages is shown on the growth charts on the following pages. Typical growth is shown by the heavy center line, and faster and slower rates by the lines above and below it. The variations in the curves show that there are periods of rapid and slow growth. After the fast growth of the first few years, the changes become more gradual and then fairly steady.

The most valuable tool for assessing children's growth is a well-kept growth chart. The most widely used charts show age marked along the bottom and height and weight marked along the sides. Children's height and weight should be measured and recorded during each visit to the physician.

Looking at growth differences

The growth patterns of boys and girls are different. In the first 2 years, boys are slightly taller than girls. After that, until puberty, their heights are similar. Girls' skeletal ages—the degree to which their bones have matured—are generally more advanced than are those of boys. Children who are overweight often grow faster and reach puberty earlier than other children.

Children's rates of growth are not even. They may vary from year to year and are often fastest in the spring and summer. For this reason, growth evaluations should extend for six months to a year.

Coping with short stature

Children who are not growing at an appropriate rate should be evaluated by their pediatricians. Some children may be short because they come from a short family, and the genetic potential for height is small.

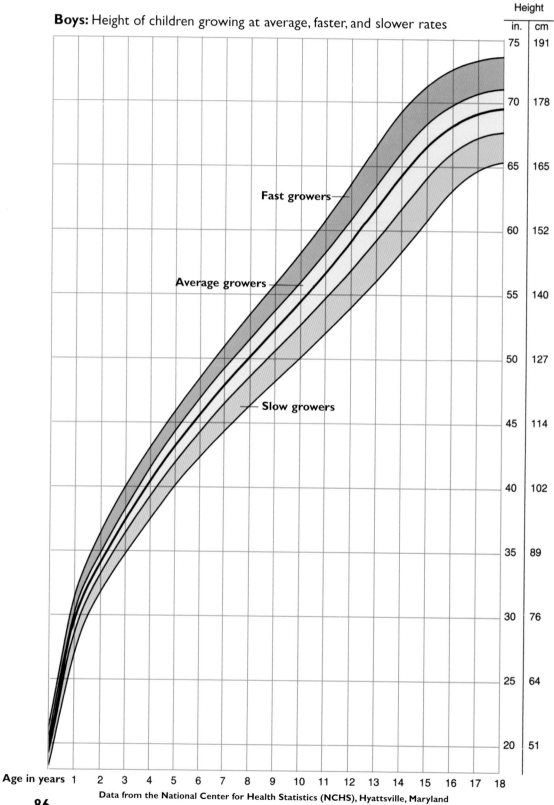

Boys: Height of children growing at average, faster, and slower rates

Height
in. | cm

Fast growers

Average growers

Slow growers

Age in years 1 2 3 4 5 6 7 8 9 10 11 12 13 14 15 16 17 18

Data from the National Center for Health Statistics (NCHS), Hyattsville, Maryland

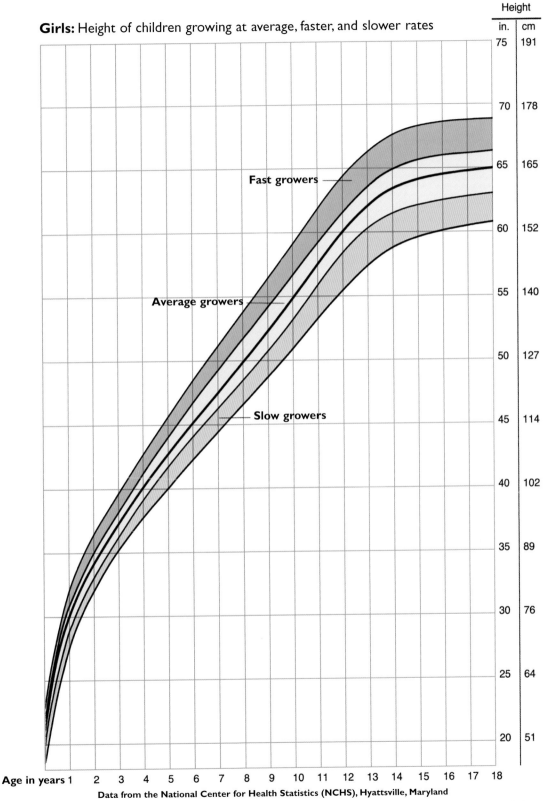

Girls: Height of children growing at average, faster, and slower rates

Height
in. | cm

Fast growers

Average growers

Slow growers

Age in years 1 2 3 4 5 6 7 8 9 10 11 12 13 14 15 16 17 18

Data from the National Center for Health Statistics (NCHS), Hyattsville, Maryland

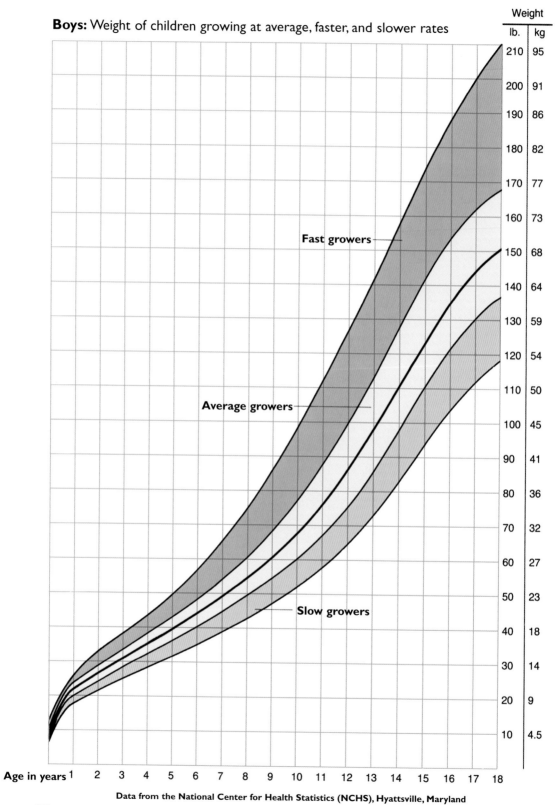

Boys: Weight of children growing at average, faster, and slower rates

Weight

lb.	kg
210	95
200	91
190	86
180	82
170	77
160	73
150	68
140	64
130	59
120	54
110	50
100	45
90	41
80	36
70	32
60	27
50	23
40	18
30	14
20	9
10	4.5

Fast growers

Average growers

Slow growers

Age in years 1 2 3 4 5 6 7 8 9 10 11 12 13 14 15 16 17 18

Data from the National Center for Health Statistics (NCHS), Hyattsville, Maryland

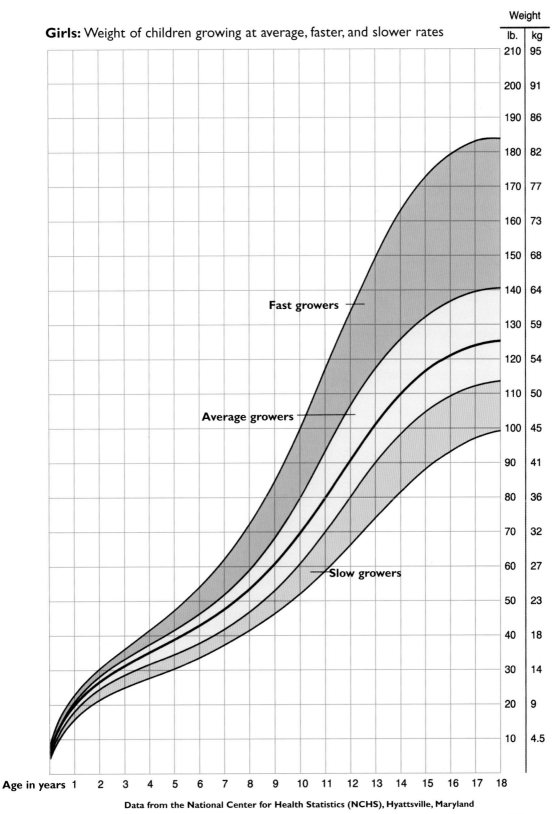

Girls: Weight of children growing at average, faster, and slower rates

Weight
| lb. | kg |

Fast growers

Average growers

Slow growers

Age in years 1 2 3 4 5 6 7 8 9 10 11 12 13 14 15 16 17 18

Data from the National Center for Health Statistics (NCHS), Hyattsville, Maryland

89

Other children have a delay in puberty or a delayed growth spurt, a condition called constitutional growth delay. These children are shorter than their peers but eventually reach normal height.

Worldwide, the most common cause of short stature is poor nutrition. A deprived environment can also cause it. Other causes include diseases of the heart, lungs, pancreas, kidneys, and digestive tract, and such endocrine disorders as a lack of thyroid hormone or a lack or partial deficiency of growth hormone. Too much cortisol, a stress hormone, also can cause short stature.

Children may be small for other reasons. Intrauterine growth retardation—slow growth before birth—may be caused by an infection during pregnancy or by a pregnant woman's use of alcohol, tobacco, or drugs. Chromosomal abnormalities can cause short stature. Skeletal abnormalities or bone disease also can affect the size and shape of bones. Occasionally the causes are not completely clear.

Therapy for short stature is directed at the underlying medical condition. Most growth hormone deficiencies can be treated by a pediatric endocrinologist. Children who are short because of delayed puberty, especially boys, also may benefit from medical intervention.

Coping with tall stature

Just as there are small children, there are about as many who are taller than most of their peers.

Most tall children have tall parents. Tall boys rarely complain about their size. However, tall girls may feel ill at ease. Our society seems to expect girls to be shorter than boys. Children who are growing abnormally fast should be checked by their pediatricians.

Abnormal height is most often caused by an endocrine disease or genetic condition. Growth hormone excess may be caused by a small tumor in the pituitary gland. A more common cause of unusually fast growth is early puberty. Genetic conditions that cause tall stature are rare, and they often include abnormal body proportions.

Dealing with emotional factors of growth

Some children with tall or short stature are emotionally troubled by their condition. Parents can boost children's self-esteem by emphasizing other characteristics, such as intelligence, personality, and talents. Children should be helped to see that their value doesn't come from height but from other qualities. Children who are very self-conscious about their size may need additional help in coping. In some cases, evaluation and treatment by a mental health professional may be necessary.

Choosing Day Care

Increasingly, parents need day care for their children while they work. Many parents are uncertain about what type of care they should seek. What day-care options are available for parents, and what are the advantages and disadvantages of each?

Types of day care for younger children

The types of day care available for younger children include day-care centers, family day care, and in-home care.

Many working parents enroll their children in a day-care center. Different day-care centers have different sponsors, including churches, schools, colleges, independent owners, chains, and employers. Regardless of what type of day-care center parents choose, there are some things to consider:

- The center should be licensed and inspected regularly for health, safety, cleanliness, staffing, and program content. Just because a day-care center is licensed does not mean it is regularly inspected. Parents should check to see how often the center had announced and unannounced inspections in the past year and what was checked. To find out about regulations in their area, parents can contact a city, county, or state department of social services.
- Caregivers and center directors should have basic training and experience in early childhood development. Parents can check to see if centers are accredited by state or national organizations.
- Age-appropriate toys, a daily schedule, and joyful interactions between children and staff should all be evident. Parents should be able to make unannounced visits to the center to see their children and should be notified promptly if their children get sick or injured.

The staff of a good day-care center has training and experience in early childhood development.

A good day-care center that meets the above criteria is often costly because its professional staff commands good wages and its material expenses are high.

Day-care centers are often open only during certain hours, are more likely to exclude ill children, and charge extra when parents are late in picking up children.

Some parents choose family day care, or day-care homes. In family day care, an adult cares for a small group of children in his or her own home. Usually, this adult is a mother with her own children. Some caregivers are licensed or registered with the state and have their home visited by an inspector. However, since many day-care homes are not regulated, there is no assurance that they meet safety and health codes. Here are some things parents can look for when considering family day care:

- Is the home clean and safe?
- Are the caregiver and the caregiver's children healthy?
- Is television watching limited to one or two hours a day?
- How does the caregiver handle meals and discipline?
- How many children, including the caregiver's children, are in the home at one time? A child-care home should not have more than six children per adult caregiver. The total number of children should be even fewer when infants and toddlers are included.
- Is there backup care for emergency situations?
- What kind of training—if any—does the caregiver have? Many home-care providers will not have any formal training, but they may have years of experience doing day care or of caring for their own children.

There are some advantages to family day care over day-care centers. It is often less expensive than day-care centers. Homes are less likely to exclude ill children and are less likely to penalize parents for picking up their children late. They are also likely to be located near the children's own homes, necessitating less travel time and fewer early-morning awakenings for sleepy children.

Most providers of family day-care homes are dedicated people who truly wish to give the best care. However, one advantage of day-care centers over family day care can be reliability. Most centers are open five days a week no matter what. Caregivers in family day-care settings may have to cancel on parents if they or one of their children become sick or if they wish to take a vacation.

Another option for day care is to hire an in-home baby sitter or nanny. In-home care can be very convenient. Many in-home caregivers can arrange their schedules to match parents' needs. Since the caregiver comes to the home, children do not have to adjust to a new setting and parents don't have to worry about travel time. Having their children at home gives parents greater control over their children's environment, as well. Also, children can receive more individual attention, especially if the caregiver is not expected to do housekeeping. In-home care may lessen children's exposure to seasonal illnesses, because they are exposed to fewer children.

Skilled in-home caregivers can be hard to find and can be expensive. And there are other considerations. Parents need to have a backup plan for times when the caregiver is sick or goes on vacation. Parents must judge the caregiver's character, health, and skill. This makes personal references very important. In some states or communities, agencies may provide training, placement, and supervision for in-home caregivers.

Which type of care is best? There is no easy answer. When choosing any kind of day care, parents should consider the following:

- **Quality of relationships.** Do the children really seem to like and enjoy the caregiver? Is the caregiver especially trained in taking care of children?

- **Location.** How far will the care be from home? From work? Is it convenient for both parents? Can both parents easily get there in an emergency?

- **Hours.** What hours of care are needed? What happens if parents are late?

- **Alternative arrangements.** What happens if children are sick? What happens if the caregiver cannot come? What if the day-care center is closed?

- **Consistency.** Are the program's policies on meals, discipline, and toilet training the same as those at home? Will children be able to have a long-term, stable relationship with the caregiver?

Choosing day care for school-age children

Some school-age children need day care before and after school. Before- and after-school programs may be located in a child's school, in a day-care center or family day-care home, or with a sitter.

Dealing with day-care problems

It is the parents' responsibility to ensure that their children receive the best care. Parents need to talk with caregivers regularly. They should plan to spend time with their children and caregivers every day, both before they leave and when they return. When problems occur, the home caregiver or staff should be able and willing to help. If problems persist, and parents suspect their child's health or safety is in question, they should find another child-care arrangement right away.

Children, Television, and the Internet

Television affects the way children spend their time and what and how they learn. Many children also spend time playing video games and using the Internet. Are these activities safe for children? What can parents do to control the influence of these activities?

Watching television

Television provides people with a wide range of new experiences. Without leaving their homes, TV viewers can see how people in far-off lands look and live. They can glimpse real-life tragedies and moments of great triumph.

While there is little agreement about how television specifically affects young people, it clearly has an impact on them. Young children, who learn by observing, will try out some of the behaviors they see on TV, both positive and negative. For this reason, children who watch programs with violent overtones tend to behave more aggressively. Children also may be influenced by the sexual behavior they see on television, adopting it at a far earlier age than their parents want.

Many social scientists believe that young people also likely form false impressions from watching a lot of television. They may come to believe in the stereotypes they see and form prejudices, or they may be disappointed in their own less-than-idyllic family life. Television rarely shows the effort that goes into successful lives, so children may not understand that success generally comes through hard work and sacrifice. It also does not help them understand the consequences of actions, including violent acts.

Aside from leaving people with unrealistic impressions, television viewing takes time from important leisure activities, such as reading, conversation, social gatherings, and exercise. Ads for products also influence children, increasing their desires for material goods.

Living with television

Parents can do a great deal to control the influence of TV on children's lives:

- Limit the amount of television children watch each day. Children need to learn that watching TV is a privilege; it is not a right.
- Forbid children to watch violent and overly sexual programming.
- Avoid using television as an electronic baby sitter. Instead parents should look for other ways to engage their children if they are busy.
- Watch television with children and take the opportunity to teach them about what they see.

Like TV watching, Internet use needs safe limits and guidance from parents.

Parents can also avoid watching a lot of television themselves. By being good role models, they can diminish television's importance in family life. It is worth the effort!

Using the Internet

The Internet is a vast computer network that connects many of the world's businesses, institutions, and people. It has made huge amounts of information accessible to more people than ever before.

While the Internet is a great tool, there are questions about children's use of it. Not all information on the Internet is accurate, and some is deliberately misleading. Many parents are concerned about violent or pornographic material. They worry about possible criminals lurking in "chat rooms," through which people send messages to each other, and seeking to arrange face-to-face meetings with unsuspecting victims.

Living with the Internet

Just as parents have rules about watching TV, it is important to have rules about using the Internet. To keep children's time on the Internet safe, productive, and fun, parents should follow these guidelines:

- Set limits on the amount of time children can spend online each day or each week.
- Do not let "surfing" the Internet take the place of homework, outdoor play, or friends.
- Make sure children know that people online are not always who they say they are and that online information is not necessarily private.
- Teach children to never give out personal information, never use a credit card online without permission, never share passwords, never arrange a face-to-face meeting, never respond to messages that make them feel confused or uncomfortable, and never use bad language or send mean messages online.
- Make a point of participating in children's online time. Stay involved and monitor what children are doing online.

Special programs known as parental control software can help parents block access to sites that may be unsuitable for children. Education associations, Internet providers, and libraries often have information on blocking software.

Moving

Moving can be an exciting adventure or a disruption in children's lives. However, since children usually follow the lead of their parents, the degree of excitement or uneasiness that children feel will depend largely on their parents' attitudes and explanations.

Most children, especially those who have close friends or who have formed strong ties to people, places, and the routines of their neighborhood, will feel sad at leaving. But beyond such normal regrets, how parents act can make children eager to tackle a new and interesting life experience.

Preparing children for a move

If children are old enough to understand, parents should talk about the move often and give as much information as possible beforehand. More lead time means more time for children to get used to the idea. Parents should answer questions completely and honestly and be receptive to children's reactions, positive or negative. It might be helpful for parents to share their own thoughts about the move, or to talk about how they handled similar experiences as young children.

If possible, parents should give children a clear picture of what it may be like to live in the new place.

If the family is planning to move to another part of the country, or to another country, parents and children can study maps and read stories and articles about the area. This will give children a better idea of where they will be living.

Parents also should discuss any aspects of the move that may present problems for children, such as a different climate or the lack of certain things they are accustomed to in their present home. Whenever possible, parents need to explain unfamiliar local customs, so that children will take an interest in the different ways people do things. These explanations will help children learn to respect differences.

Children's reactions to moving are likely to mirror their parents' feelings.

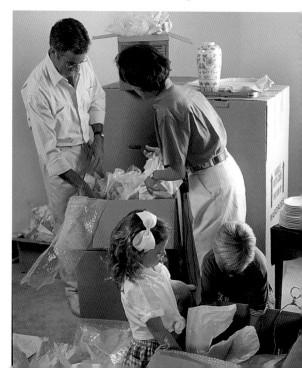

Involving children in planning and decision-making—to an appropriate extent—can help them feel that they are participating in the move rather than having it forced upon them.

Coping with problems

Even with the best preparation, some children may have deep emotional reactions to moving. Often, anxiety over the welfare of a pet that cannot be taken along may precipitate an emotional crisis. Parents can relieve anxiety by allowing children to help find a good home for the pet.

Leaving friends may be especially hard on children. Joining small community or religious groups that usually welcome newcomers may help children feel more at ease. Many people have had some experience with moving to a new community, and they expect to welcome newcomers. The friendly atmosphere makes it easier for children to meet new friends and develop new interests.

If children are shy or timid or show much uneasiness, they will need a lot of support when they enter a new school. Parents should take children to school before classes begin and introduce them to the principal, teachers, and if possible, some future classmates. If children have problems with schoolwork or physical problems such as poor coordination, vision, or hearing, the school should know about them. The school should also know about

children's abilities. Most teachers want to be helpful, but to do their best, they must be aware of special needs.

Sometimes children appear to have adjusted to a move without difficulty, but they have an emotional slump after the initial excitement has worn off. Perhaps the new school is not as challenging or as stimulating as the old school, and children are bored. Or perhaps it is quite a bit more challenging than the previous one, and children have trouble keeping up. Or they could find it hard to make new friends. Parents can help by talking to teachers and school counselors. Together, they might be able to help children adjust by helping them find more interests or more congenial friends.

It is not unusual for well-adjusted children to feel lonely, restless, and moody after a move. But if children were already unhappy, the move may increase their anxiety. Parents may have to turn to someone trained to help them understand the basic causes of their children's unhappiness.

Most children, however, settle into the new community within a period of months. Their adjustment is helped considerably if the experience of the move has given them the secure feeling that wherever they live, their family can make a home under all kinds of circumstances. This is a fine way to establish the emotional security that will support them throughout life.

Traveling with Young Children

A family vacation is a special time, but it may take some creativity to make getting there fun for children. Parents can plan some activities to help keep children contented on a long trip.

- If the trip is long, start at a time when children will be likely to sleep for all or part of the trip.
- Pack activities to pass the time. Paper and crayons or markers for drawing are favorites with most children. A tray with legs will make them easier for children to use. A tray also comes in handy for doing jigsaw puzzles and for building with blocks.
- Bring a small cassette recorder along with some favorite music and story tapes. Children also love blank tapes for recording songs they sing or stories they make up along the way.
- Play games. Many popular children's games come in travel-sized

Buckling up is a good start to any vacation trip.

editions, and card games are easy to take along.

- Prepare a list of things children can look for along the ride, and see how many they can find.
- Take along small surprises for children to open and play with as a reward for behaving well.
- When traveling by car, plan to stop every few hours to allow children to run off pent-up energy. Knowing that there will be frequent breaks will help children remain safely seated. One of the most difficult parts of traveling with children is having to confine them to their car seats or seat belts, but remember that "buckling up" is the only safe way to travel on both short and long trips.
- Pack favorite snack foods such as dry cereal, pretzels, raisins, and juice. If the weather is nice, pack a picnic lunch and plan to stop at an outdoor rest area, where children can run around and burn off some energy.
- Bring moist wipes for a quick, sanitary clean-up; a change of clothes in case the traveling clothes become particularly messy; and a favorite stuffed animal or blanket for comfort.
- Always have a first-aid kit while traveling. Childhood accidents occur when traveling because of changes in routine and environ-

ment. Items to bring along include bandages, an antibiotic spray, acetaminophen, and important health information, such as a list of allergies, other medical conditions, or regular medication.

- If traveling by plane, plan to take a nonstop flight and request seats in the first row or on the aisle, where there is more room. Although airlines usually provide earlier boarding for those flying with children, this may not be the best option with active infants or toddlers because they will be confined longer. It may be better to board later and let children run off energy. During take-off and landing, encourage children to drink liquids or chew gum (if age-appropriate) to equalize pressure and prevent ear discomfort. If children are prone to ear infections, have their ears checked before flying.

Children are usually thrilled about traveling and going on a vacation, but parents need to keep in mind that changes in children's routines, coupled with added excitement, may alter their sleeping patterns and also cause changes in their behavior. However, these are temporary disruptions and should not interfere with the fun of a family vacation. Life will go back to normal after returning home.

Protecting Children from Poisons

Children explore their environment by touching, smelling, and tasting. They often don't pause to consider whether or not something is good for them. They just try it. So it is not surprising that every year, hospitals treat thousands of children who have ingested harmful substances.

Cosmetics are the leading poisonous substance ingested by small children. Other leading substances, in order, are plants, soaps and detergents, cold medications, analgesics, and vitamins. Child-resistant packaging on some household items has helped prevent some poisonings. Unfortunately, no packaging is absolutely childproof.

Observing some safety rules, and checking or cleaning out areas of the house, can help protect children from poisoning. Here are some rules to follow and tips for ways to make the home safer:

- Keep all medicines and chemicals out of the reach of children. Discard any potential poisons that are of little use. Children are more sensitive than adults to poison, and a smaller amount may cause death. Store all aftershaves, colognes, and perfumes—which have a high alcohol content—and all super glues out of reach.
- Don't refer to medication as candy.
- Buy medications and household products with child-resistant caps.
- Never leave alcoholic beverages within children's reach.
- Always read the warning labels on hazardous products.
- Keep all products in their original containers and avoid purchasing toxic substances, such as household cleaners, that have appealing fragrances like lemon or almond.
- Never put inedible or hazardous products in cups or other containers that would normally be used for food or beverages.
- Avoid taking medication in the presence of children.
- Teach preschoolers not to eat or drink anything unless it is given to them by an adult they know.
- Do not depend on close adult supervision to keep children safe. Children move quickly and can get into things before an adult can intervene.
- Be alert for repeat occurrences. For some reason, children exposed to dangerous substances or poisoning are likely to try a second ingestion within one year.
- Keep toxic plants out of reach.
- Maintain the furnace in good working order. This will help prevent both natural gas and carbon monoxide poisoning.
- Keep the telephone numbers of physicians, hospital emergency rooms, and poison control centers near your telephone.

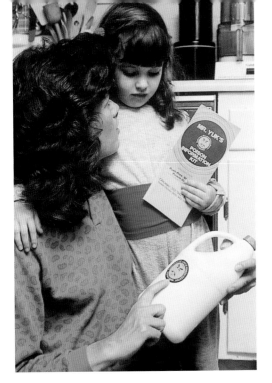

Parents should teach children to recognize poisonous substances. Danger symbols on containers can help.

- If children swallow a nonfood item or are exposed to toxic fumes, call a doctor, hospital, or poison control center. Make sure to have the container handy in case there are questions about the substance. Poison control centers furnish first-aid information and advice when children have swallowed poisons. However, not all areas have them. If your area has none, call a doctor or hospital.
- Do not attempt self-directed home treatment of poisoned children. In some cases, inducing vomiting can worsen the condition. Do not rely on a poison treatment chart. Call a doctor, hospital, or poison control center.
- Keep a one-ounce bottle of syrup of ipecac in the home medicine

chest. This is used to induce vomiting in some poisoning situations. However, do not use syrup of ipecac without professional advice.
- If you are unsure what caused the poisoning, save any vomit or urine children produce. A hospital may need to analyze it.

One situation for which adults should begin treatment before seeking professional help is eye contamination. An eye exposed to an irritant should be flushed with lukewarm water for 15 minutes. The quickest method is to use a gentle stream of lukewarm water from a kitchen or bathroom faucet. Another method is to use a pitcher and slowly pour water over the eye. If children fight the treatment, wrap them in a blanket or sheet to keep them from struggling.

Another area in which treatment can be given before calling for professional assistance is skin exposed to acids, alkalis, petroleum products, or insecticides. Remove children's clothing and bathe them thoroughly. Discard any leather or other porous materials that could have absorbed the substance.

Remember, almost all nonfood substances are a potential danger to children. Keeping dangerous substances out of sight and out of reach goes a long way in protecting children against accidental poisoning.

Explaining Death to Children

Almost all children at some point ask, "What does it mean to be dead?" or "Will I die, too?" Children may want to know why and how a pet dies. They may have seen a funeral procession or heard about the death of a well-known person. Or a family member may have died.

Many parents who are willing and able to discuss almost any subject with their children become evasive and ill at ease when questioned about death. Perhaps it is because most of us would rather not think about death. But when a loved one dies, it is important that parents be prepared to talk about it.

Children usually have strong emotions about death. They may have feelings of sorrow, fear, resentment, and even guilt. They may become confused and bewildered. How parents explain death, and how they answer children's questions about death, are important. Parents should be aware that children's concepts of death change as they get older.

Between 3 and 5, children tend to think of death as a journey from which a person will soon return. Or, they may think death is a kind of going to sleep and then waking up. When told of a death, they may express sorrow but seem to forget about it soon afterward. Parents who are unaware of this common reaction may worry that children are self-centered and heartless.

Between the ages of 5 and 9, most children accept the idea that death is irreversible, but they believe that death happens only to certain people. Around the ages of 9 or 10, children begin to understand that death happens to all living things, and they will die eventually, too.

Answering questions

No matter how difficult it may be, an open, calm answer about death is the best one. Children are not nearly as afraid of what they can understand as they are of things that are cloaked in mystery.

In explaining death, parents usually have to deal with such facts as illness, accidents, or old age. The amount of information should relate to a child's capacity to understand. For instance, if a 3-year-old wants to know why a grandparent has died, it is usually enough to say, "She was very old and very tired." A 6-year-old might be told that the grandmother was very old and tired, and that eventually everyone grows old and tired and can no longer go on living.

Some parents give evasive answers in the belief that they are guarding against pain that the truth would cause. But an evasive answer may cause problems. For example,

When a loved one dies, children need to be able to talk about their feelings.

when a grandfather dies and a 6-year-old is told that he went to sleep, the child may become fearful of going to sleep and not waking up.

Even a religious explanation is not always helpful. Few children find comfort in such explanations as "God took him." They could have feelings of resentment against God.

Children often feel that in some way or other they are responsible for the death. Parents can help children overcome such guilt.

Children are more deeply affected by some deaths than by others. When a playmate or a playmate's parent dies, children are likely to think that they might also die young or lose a parent. Parents can reassure children by stressing that few people die young. Parents also might add that friends and family will take care of their children should anything happen to them.

The death of a parent is especially difficult. Children suffer not only grief, but a loss of security. If surviving parents are in no condition to comfort children, they may feel rejected. At such times, adult relatives or friends of the family can be a source of strength and reassurance about the future. At no time should a child be told that he or she must take on adult responsibilities to make up for the absent parent.

Mourning

There are differences of opinion about children's participation in family gatherings of mourning and funeral ceremonies. A common practice in many families is to send the children to stay with friends so that they will be spared the effects of grief. In some instances, this may be wise, but often it makes children feel alone and shut out. To be with the family, yet to be protected from extreme demonstrations of grief, is often more reassuring for children than being spared the experience.

Parents faced with helping children understand a death in the family or the death of a close friend should be honest. They need to help children see that life holds some sorrow as well as joy for everyone. Children need love, affection, and understanding to get through the experience in a positive way. The value of the feeling of belonging, in sorrow as well as in joy, cannot be overemphasized.

Dealing with Behavior Problems

At times, all children behave in ways that puzzle or worry parents. Many children may even show what seem to be symptoms of a behavior problem. Symptoms such as aggressiveness, fears, and compulsions indicate a behavior problem only when they are severe or occur frequently. Such severe problems are typically the result of some sort of emotional disturbance. However, before parents conclude that this is the case, they should make sure that their children do not have a physical or mental illness. Many symptoms of behavior problems can be created or made worse by a physical or mental illness.

Understanding emotional problems

Children live in four different worlds—the world of family and home; the world of school; the world of friendships; and their inner world. Behavior problems can occur as a result of emotional problems in all or any of these four worlds.

In the home, there is normally is a bond of affection between parents, and between children and each parent. As a part of the family, children are expected to pay a reasonable amount of attention to family rules and to perform tasks that are appropriate for their age and ability. Emotional problems may develop if there is not a good relationship with parents, if independence proceeds too slowly or too rapidly, or if family rules and tasks are ignored. Although quarreling and jealousy between siblings are hard to take, most child development specialists typically view them as a normal part of sibling relationships.

Children spend a great deal of time in the world of school—about 1,000 hours a year. There, they are expected to perform to the best of their ability, conform socially, and develop interests in studies and other activities. Emotional problems can occur if children's performance in school does not match the expectations of parents, and in turn, the parents pressure their children to improve. The emotional problems may result in a disinterest in school. Children may start to dislike school, act out in the classroom, or fail to achieve their potential.

Childhood friendships have a tremendous impact on children's development. From such associations, children learn social customs and patterns of behavior. Much of the ability to succeed in adult relationships grows out of the behavior patterns that are developed during childhood. Because of the importance of healthy childhood friendships, parents should be concerned about children who are always

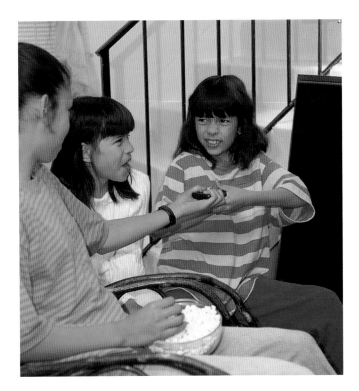

Some squabbling between brothers and sisters is normal, even in close and affectionate families.

alone or who are consistently aggressive toward other children. Such behaviors could signal an emotional problem.

The inner world of children is in some ways the most important and the most difficult to understand. This is their world of thoughts, fears, hopes, attitudes, and ambitions. When children have a strong, constant sense of not measuring up to other children, it is reasonable to assume that there may be an emotional problem.

Everyone has to face problems of one kind or another throughout life. In spite of this, well-adjusted people continue to find life a source of satisfaction. Such people are usually optimistic about the future. If this feeling of optimism never

occurs in children, then emotional problems result.

Two of the most common behavior problems in children are unrealistic fears and aggressive behavior.

All children are afraid from time to time. Fear is a normal emotion. However, fears are unrealistic if they occur regularly in the absence of real danger. In some cases, such fears may be directly related to a frightening past experience. In other cases, they may be only indirectly related to a past event. For example, a child who feels extreme guilt may expect severe punishment and then develop an abnormal fear of death, accidents, or illness. Some fears become so intense that they prevent children from carrying out normal activities.

Psychologists define aggression as angry, hostile behavior that is intended to hurt or upset others. Such behavior in young children can result from frustration. Children may feel frustrated if their demands are not met or if their feelings of worthiness are threatened. If the anger is intense, it may erupt into a tantrum—a common form of aggression in young children.

Other special problems of childhood also may be symptoms of emotional or physical disorders. They include hyperactivity (extreme restlessness), extreme shyness, and bed-wetting.

Finding the root of problems

If children frequently show symptoms of a behavior disorder, parents should not ignore the symptoms and hope they will disappear in time. Children are too important for parents to rely on chance.

If their children are having behavior problems, parents need to discuss it together. It is extremely important that the discussion take place when they are feeling good rather than when they are upset and angry because their children have behaved poorly. During the discussion, they must take a look at how their family as a group and how each individual member behaves in relation to their child with the behavior problem.

Also, parents must be able to admit that while the ways they do things may work well with some children, and may even be necessary, they have not been successful with the emotionally disturbed child. This admission calls for a willingness to accept the fact that their parental behavior is related to the child's difficulty, and that a change in their approach may be a solution to the problem.

There are certain types of parental behavior that can lead to behavior problems in children. A few are listed below. Some problems, however, have no obvious cause. Some simply stem from children's personalities. Some children become more frustrated than others and act out in different ways. Some problems are caused by a chemical imbalance that medication may be able to help. Because there are many causes, consulting a health care professional is always a good idea.

Demanding perfection. Parents who demand a great deal of themselves may place unreasonable demands on their children. No matter how hard children try, their perfectionist parents are never quite satisfied or pleased. Emotional problems can often be related to this abnormal demand for perfection. Perfectionist parents should try to be less rigid about rules and look for behaviors that can be praised.

Being inconsistent. Inconsistent parents create an uncertain environment by changing rules so often that children cannot know what is expected. Most parents are inconsistent at times, but when they constantly change rules relating to children's behavior, it is damaging to the children. Children thrive on consistency. Inconsistent parents should decide important basic household rules, write them down, and try to stick to them.

Overprotecting children.
Overprotective parents shield children excessively, either because they cannot bear their children growing up or because of their own concern for dangers in the world. This attitude may inhibit the development of independent skills. Parents who recognize that overprotection is a problem should talk to other parents and child development experts about ways to allow children more independence.

Being indulgent. Never setting limits may also be a source of a behavior disorder. Children are much more comfortable when they have rules to follow. Rules prepare them to face the many situations in which individual desires must be put aside in favor of group needs.

Quarreling. Parents also may contribute to children's problems if there is constant quarreling. The obvious solution is to avoid quarreling in the presence of children.

Being uninvolved. Parents who have little to do with their children will be unable to convince their children of their love, interest, and concern. Children need models after which they can pattern their own behavior. To be effective models, parents must be available and interested in their children. Adults who rely heavily on punishment may tend to deal with recurring problems by thinking up new and unusual punishments. If children show symptoms of a behavior problem and have been punished a great deal, it is reasonable to assume that more punishment will only aggravate the condition. If punishment is necessary, parents should make sure that the punishment is not excessive. In addition, parents should also be sure to offer a lot of praise to reinforce good behavior.

Working with children with behavior problems. If parents recognize that previous methods of handling their children have been unsuccessful or even harmful, they should plan a new program. If the children are old enough to reason with, the process will be made easier by a frank discussion when all are feeling friendly. Parents should tell their children how concerned they are and how much they want to help. They should indicate how they plan to change their behavior, and they should agree to meet on a regular basis to discuss progress. The children should be allowed to speak freely during the discussions, and nothing they say should be held against them.

If the children's behavior has become a problem at school, it is important that parents discuss the problem with teachers and other staff, such as the principal, counselor, social worker, or nurse. These people are interested in the children and can offer advice and guidance. This may be extremely valuable in helping parents understand why their children are having difficulty.

Seeking professional help

It is usually difficult for parents to admit that their children may need psychological support. It is reasonable for parents to assume that they can work out some of their children's problems without outside help. If there is improvement, they should continue. However, if in a reasonable time there is no improvement, it is time to seek professional help.

If children are overly fearful or aggressive, or show such symptoms as continued hyperactivity, extreme shyness, or bed-wetting, parents should consult their pediatrician or family doctor. If necessary, they will be referred to a psychiatrist, a clinical psychologist, or a mental health clinic. Often an outsider with specialized training can approach the problem with greater objectivity.

When parents seek help for their children, they must be prepared to accept the fact that they may be partly responsible for the emotional problem. Parents should be willing to learn how they have contributed to the problem and work with the doctor to produce good results.

The treatment of children with behavior problems often requires a great deal of time and patience on the part of parents and child guidance specialists. A severe behavioral problem usually takes a long time to develop, and as long a time may be required to correct it. Fortunately, most children respond favorably to treatment, especially when all members of the family are trying to help.

Learning Disabilities

Children are born with unique developmental profiles and can exhibit strengths and weaknesses in different aspects of development, such as fine and gross motor activity, attention span, memory function, language, perception, and productivity. Weaknesses in any of these areas may affect the ability of children to function well in a regular classroom environment. Such mild impairments in child development are often identified as learning disabilities. They are often first noted when children enter school and have trouble meeting the academic and social challenges of their new environment.

Learning disabilities may be expressed in a variety of symptoms, and at times it is difficult to distinguish between normal variations in children's learning styles and true learning disabilities.

Certain risk factors may predispose children to learning difficulties. Some children may have a genetic abnormality. Others may have experienced serious medical problems that damaged the central nervous system and, therefore, affected their development.

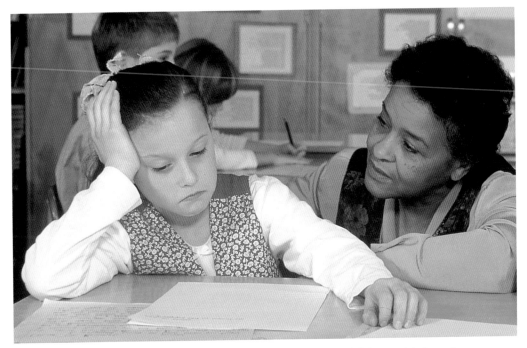

To overcome the fear of "looking bad" in the classroom, children with learning disabilities need steady support and encouragement from parents and teachers.

Exposure to toxins and infections can sometimes adversely affect the development of children's central nervous system before birth. With the vast majority of children, however, the cause of the learning disability is not easily identified.

Developmental skills

In order to function well in school, children must acquire a variety of developmental skills, including auditory and visual memory, expressive and receptive language, motor skills, attention, higher order reasoning, and motivation. The presence or absence of these skills in the developmental profile of children can affect their performance in such academic areas as reading, spelling, science, mathematics, as well as social development.

The desire to be accepted by other children in the classroom is an important goal for most school-aged children. When children enter school, they leave the security of the home for an environment where they face peer pressure every day. For most children, this change produces positive results. By interacting with other children in this new environment, they learn more about themselves, as well as about patterns of socially acceptable behavior. But for children with learning disabilities, the change can be painful. Their main goal in the classroom is not to be embarrassed by their performance. "Looking bad" can cause children with learning disabilities to lose confidence in their abilities and lose self-esteem.

Children who constantly experience failure in the classroom express their frustration and unhappiness in different ways. Some children become socially withdrawn and depressed. Others may act out in class. Children also may experience such symptoms as headaches, stomachaches, limb pains, nail biting, and wetting or soiling their pants.

Dealing with learning disabilities

The parents' observations of their children's development in the years before school begins are often important in identifying children who may be at risk for school failure. Children who are delayed in reaching developmental milestones, especially in language skills, are more likely to have problems in school. Parents who feel that their children have marked developmental delays in language skills, attention, and such basic self-help skills as dressing, should contact their pediatrician. Early identification and intervention can help such children develop their full capabilities.

In most cases, however, the problems of children with learning disabilities do not become obvious until the children are in school. Teachers' concerns about children's difficulties in paying attention or learning a specific skill, such as recognizing letters, may be the parents' first clue that learning disabilities exist. If children are unable to master skills that are readily learned by classmates, a complete evaluation should be performed. This evaluation should include tests to identify the developmental skills needed to function efficiently in a classroom setting. Children should also have a physical examination, including vision and hearing screening, in order to rule out any medical causes of learning impairments. A social evaluation also should be included, since environmental factors also may affect performance.

When the evaluation is completed, parents and teachers can be provided with a description of children's developmental strengths and weaknesses, and recommendations can be made for an appropriate classroom environment and for changes in the home that would benefit children as well.

Medications are sometimes prescribed as part of the treatment of children with an attention deficit disorder (ADD), or attention deficit/hyperactivity disorder (ADHD). It is important for parents and teachers to understand that medications will not cure a learning disability, even though they sometimes help children who have serious problems with inattention and impulsive behavior. Counseling for children and family is also sometimes recommended in order to help children deal with problems as they are encountered. With these kinds of support, and with continued observation and help, children with learning disabilities can be expected to develop academically and socially to their full capabilities.

Mental Retardation

The term "mental retardation" refers to a condition in which people have substantial limitations in their intellectual abilities. Children are diagnosed as mentally retarded if they perform far below average, both intellectually and behaviorally. They do not think, reason, remember, and learn as well as other children the same age. However, except in cases of extreme retardation, parents and teachers can help children with mental retardation develop strategies so that they need not be totally dependent on others to survive. The way the family and others treat children with mental retardation has a lot to do with whether or not they can remain emotionally healthy and well adjusted.

Mental retardation can result from any factor that hinders healthy brain development. Babies may be mentally retarded as a result of genetic errors that may or may not have been inherited or as a result of an accident that results in brain injury. Consumption of alcohol during pregnancy can lead to a condition in babies called fetal alcohol syndrome, which can cause mental retardation. Use of prescription, nonprescription, or illegal drugs also can harm developing babies' brains. Exposure before birth to certain infections, including rubella (also called German measles) and

HIV, also can cause retardation. During childhood, retardation can result from such causes as brain infections, head injuries, prolonged high fevers, or lead poisoning.

To be considered mentally retarded, people must show signs of the condition before they reach 18 years of age. The most common symptom of retardation is a delay in achieving milestones of development. Many children with severe mental retardation fail to sit up or walk at the usual age for these accomplish-

A climate of family love and support is important for all children.

ments. Children with less severe retardation may be slow in learning to talk. Mild retardation may escape detection until a child starts school and has trouble learning.

Coping with mental retardation

Whenever parents are puzzled by their children's development, they should seek professional help. The family doctor or pediatrician can refer parents to a special clinic for a detailed diagnosis and evaluation of children's conditions. As a rule, a good diagnosis will include a thorough study of physical, psychological, and social factors involved in behavior. When a thorough study has been made, parents feel less compelled to go from one doctor to another in the hope of finding an easy cure for the condition.

Children with mental retardation, like any children, should get good medical care and attention. They need nourishing food, plenty of sleep, immunizations, correction of any physical defects that can be corrected, and careful nursing during illness. A periodic reassessment of their condition is important.

Few parents adjust easily to the idea that their children are mentally retarded. Many parents find that talking to others in the same situation can be a great comfort. Through certain agencies and associations, parents meet to exchange ideas, discuss problems, set up camps or schools, and promote understanding of mental retardation.

Living with retarded children

Children with mental retardation, like all children, need to begin life with parental love in family surroundings. Today there is greater understanding of retardation and more help available in the community. Most experts recommend keeping children with mental retardation at home rather than in an institution. If parents can help them do more and more alone, they will begin to take pride and joy in their children's accomplishments, no matter how small.

The lives of children with mental retardation should be kept simple and orderly. They need to know what is expected every day. Patient teaching is required to help them learn what average children of their age learn quickly. Parents may have to repeat the same instructions, activities, and simple lessons many times before a simple idea is grasped. But children with mental retardation should not be pushed beyond their abilities. If overloaded, they may become confused, and any efforts to learn will be blocked.

Parents need patience to discipline children with mental retardation. These children need to learn rules, but what is expected should be based on their ability and development. Sometimes, parents demand better behavior from children with mental retardation than from the other children in the family. They expect far more in the way of control and cooperation than the children can possibly offer. As with any other aspect of learning, the demand for more than the children are capable of giving will hinder rather than help.

Understanding the impact on the family

While it is not always the case, the severity of children's retardation may determine the effect their disability has on the rest of their family. If the retardation is severe, it may be necessary to leave children with mental retardation in the care of sitters on occasion so that the rest of the family can get out. The other children may become resentful if their activities are curtailed by the needs of their sibling with mental retardation.

It is a good idea for parents to train special caretakers and to keep the same ones, if possible. Students who are enrolled in special education courses at nearby colleges are often attuned to young children's needs and eager to gain first-hand experience in caring for children with mental retardation.

Usually, brothers and sisters reflect the attitudes and behavior of parents toward children with mental retardation. Children with mental retardation can become scapegoats for many family problems, including problems that would exist even if the children with mental retardation were not around. Under such circumstances, a child with mental retardation will very likely not develop his or her full potential, intellectually or socially, and will have difficulty learning the skills needed to achieve some measure of independence.

On the other hand, children with mental retardation can become valued members of families, around whose needs other family members can rally and become united more strongly than ever. A child with mental retardation who is respected by parents, brothers and sisters, and relatives can return affection and develop rewarding relationships with family and friends. In such a climate of family support, the child will be able to develop social skills more fully and feel more positive about his or her very real and very important achievements.

Physical Disabilities

Physical disabilities are physical problems that will ultimately interfere with peoples' expectations, job performance, or relationships with their family, friends, and society in general. Some physically disabled children with normal intelligence have a good chance for a useful and satisfying life. The role of parents in helping ensure their children with physical disabilities have a satisfying life is to love and accept them. They must also help them develop self-confidence by concentrating on what they can do rather than on what they cannot do.

Caring for the disabled child at home

Physically disabled children have needs that go beyond special medical attention to their physical problems. Disabled children, like normal children, need good nutrition and immunization against disease. These children need periodic visits to the family doctor or the pediatrician. Babies with disabilities need the same amount of cuddling and attention as normal babies. Toddlers need to explore, and preschoolers should be stimulated with new experiences.

Children with disabilities, like normal children, must be given responsibilities and tasks appropriate to their age and abilities. This gives them the feeling of being trusted and needed. They also need discipline—neither more nor less than that needed by all children—to learn the limits of socially acceptable behavior. Children with disabilities feel more secure knowing that they are expected to be as well behaved as all other children are.

Parents should refrain from rushing to help their disabled children do things that the children can do alone. But there is no harm in making things easier for them. For instance, parents can alter clothing so that children can dress and undress with as little difficulty as possible. They can arrange furniture so that the children can get around the house more easily.

Educating children with disabilities

Medical treatment and special education during early childhood help many children with physical disabilities lessen or even overcome their disabilities. For example, special education can give the child with cerebral palsy a chance to improve coordination and speech. A school environment also provides the opportunity for children with physical disabilities to relate to people outside the family and to learn to handle other reactions to their physical differences.

Many physically disabled children attend regular classes and school activities.

Some children with physical disabilities can attend regular classes in private or public school. Some public schools have classrooms adapted to their special needs and trained teachers to instruct them. Some communities provide bus service for children who need wheelchairs, braces, or other equipment to get around.

When children are too severely disabled to attend school, public schools may send teachers to their homes, or they may provide electronic or other teaching equipment. Residential schools may provide medical and educational services in cases where parents are unable to cope with disabled children at home, or where local facilities are either inadequate or nonexistent. Such schools are very much like boarding schools in that the children may return home for holidays and other school vacations.

Finding help

The cost of providing treatment and special education for children with physical disabilities can become a financial burden. Many places have government agencies that can help. Some offer financial assistance or help in planning education.

There are many agencies and groups that deal with children with disabilities. They often offer parent-education programs to help parents face problems, understand their own attitudes, and understand the causes and the nature of their children's disabilities. Perhaps more important, parents learn they are not alone when they share their experiences with other parents of children with disabilities.

Parent-education programs are led by qualified people in the fields of medicine and special education. Discussions, lectures, visual aids, and trips to schools and institutions for people with disabilities give parents information on the health care, discipline, and physical and psychological adjustments that are necessary in caring for children with a disability. Where such groups do not exist, some agencies have mobile units to provide parents with counseling. In time, parents become aware that their disabled children are in most ways like all other children.

Resources for Parents

There are many agencies that provide information and counseling to anyone seeking help with special problems relating to family and child health and education. Some of these agencies and organizations are privately sponsored. Others are sponsored by governments. Many of them offer pamphlets and other literature on a wide variety of topics.

Telephone directories usually list local agencies and organizations. You also can find information about local and national organizations that offer information and assistance on the Internet.

If you have difficulty finding an agency or an organization that seems equipped to meet your special needs, your doctor, the nearest hospital, the local health department, or your spiritual adviser may be able to suggest others.

A great many people have had a great deal to say about child development and related subjects dealing with child guidance, family living and the changing family, education, sex education, special needs, and health.

On November 20, 1989, the United Nations General Assembly addressed these concerns and the needs of children when it adopted the Convention on the Rights of the Child. On the next two pages is a plain language version of the official text, prepared by The Save The Children Fund and UNICEF, the United Nations Children's Fund.

The Convention on the Rights of the Child

Article 1: The Convention defines a child as a person under 18 unless national law recognizes that the age of majority is reached earlier.

Article 2: All the rights laid down in the Convention are to be enjoyed by children regardless of race, color, sex, language, religion, political, or other opinion, national, ethnic, or social origin, property, disability, birth, or other status.

Article 3: All sections concerning the child should be in her/his best interests.

Article 4: The State's obligation to translate the rights of the Convention into reality.

Article 5: The State should respect the rights and responsibilities of parents to provide guidance appropriate to the child's capacities.

Article 6: The right to life.

Article 7: The right to a name and a nationality and, as far as possible, the right to know and to be cared for by her/his parents.

Article 8: The right to protection of her/his identity by the State.

Article 9: The right to live with her/his parents unless incompatible with her/his best interests. The right, if desired, to maintain personal relations and direct contact with both parents if separated from one or both.

Article 10: The right to leave and enter her/his own country, and other countries, for purposes of reunion with parents and maintaining the child-parent relationship.

Article 11: The right to protection by the State if unlawfully taken or kept abroad by a parent.

Article 12: The right to freely express an opinion in all matters affecting her/him and to have that opinion taken into account.

Article 13: The right to express views, and obtain and transmit ideas and information regardless of frontiers.

Article 14: The right to freedom of thought, conscience, and religion, subject to appropriate parental guidance.

Article 15: The right to meet together with other children and join and form associations.

Article 16: The right to protection from arbitrary and unlawful interference with privacy, family, home, and correspondence, and from libel and slander.

Article 17: The right of access to information and materials from a diversity of sources and of protection from harmful materials.

Article 18: The right to benefit from child-rearing assistance and child-care services and facilities provided to parents/guardians by the State.

Article 19: The right to protection from maltreatment by parents or others responsible for her/his care.

Article 20: The right to special protection if s/he is temporarily or permanently deprived of her/his family environment, due regard being paid to her/his cultural background.

Article 21: The right, in countries where adoption is allowed, to have it ensured that an adoption is carried out in her/his best interests.

Article 22: The right, if a refugee, to special protection.

Article 23: The right, if disabled, to special care, education, and training to help her/him enjoy a full life in conditions that ensure dignity and promote self-reliance and a full and active life in society.

Article 24: The right to the highest standard of health and medical care attainable.

Article 25: The right, if placed by the State for purposes of care, protection, or treatment, to have all aspects of that placement regularly evaluated.

Article 26: The right to benefit from social security.

Article 27: The right to a standard of living adequate for her/his physical, mental, spiritual, moral, and social development.

Article 28: The right to education, including free primary education. Discipline to be consistent with a child's human dignity.

Article 29: The right to an education that prepares her/him for an active, responsible life as an adult in a free society which respects others and the environment.

Article 30: The right, if a member of a minority community or indigenous people, to enjoy her/his own culture, to practice her/his own religion, and to use her/his own language.

Article 31: The right to rest and leisure, to engage in play, and to participate in recreational, cultural, and artistic activities.

Article 32: The right to protection from economic exploitation and work that is hazardous, interferes with her/his education, or harms her/his

health or physical, mental, spiritual, moral, and social development.

Article 33: The right to protection from narcotic drugs and from being involved in their production or distribution.

Article 34: The right to protection from sexual exploitation and abuse.

Article 35: The right to protection from being abducted, sold, or trafficked.

Article 36: The right to protection from all other forms of exploitation.

Article 37: The right not to be subjected to torture or degrading treatment. If detained, not to be kept with adults, sentenced to death, nor imprisoned for life without the possibility of release. The right to legal assistance and contact with family.

Article 38: The right, if below 15 years of age, not to be recruited into armed forces nor to engage in direct hostilities.

Article 39: The right, if the victim of armed conflict, torture, neglect, maltreatment, or exploitation, to receive appropriate treatment for her/his physical and psychological recovery and reintegration into society.

Article 40: The right, if accused or guilty of committing an offense, to age-appropriate treatment likely to promote her/his sense of dignity and worth and her/his reintegration as a constructive member of society.

Article 42: The right to be informed of these principles and provisions by the state in which s/he lives.

Note: The Convention has 54 Articles in all. Articles 41 and 43 to 54 are concerned with its implementation and entry into force.

How to Use the Index

This general index is a key to all of the material in volumes 1 through 15 of *Childcraft*. The thousands of pages in *Childcraft* are filled with information on many subjects, in both text and pictures. Often, different aspects of a subject are covered in more than one volume. Although each volume has its own index, this general index is the only place to learn where in *Childcraft* you can find all the information on a subject.

The illustration on the opposite page shows the special features used in the general index and in the individual volume indexes. To make the best use of the indexes, you should be aware of these features.

An entry is in dark type. It can be the name of a person (**Daimler, Gottlieb**), a place (**Damascus**), a thing (**dandelion**), or a general topic. Many entries are subdivided to help you locate quickly the exact information you are looking for. One feature especially helpful for children is the use of an identifier in parentheses after many of the entries, such as **date** (fruit). One entry that parents and teachers will find particularly helpful is **activities**. It lists all of the Try This! projects, games, and exercises in the set, grouping them under several broad subheadings that correspond

roughly to a breakdown by volume. This entry is found only in this volume and not in the individual indexes.

Cross-references guide you to additional headings and preferred headings. For example, if you are looking for information about day and night, the cross-reference *see also* **night, poems about,** tells you to look under that heading also. If you are looking for information about Leonardo da Vinci, the cross-reference **da Vinci, Leonardo,** *see* **Leonardo da Vinci** tells you where to look for the information.

The entries are arranged in alphabetical order. Some entries are inverted (**EDSA Revolution, Anniversary of**), so that the key portion of the entry is alphabetized.

The numbers following an entry or subentry (**15**/120) give the volume number in dark type and the page number or numbers in regular type. When there are references to more than one volume, the volumes are listed in numerical order.

If there is information in both words and pictures, the words *(with pictures)* appear after the page number or numbers. If the reference is to a picture only, the word *(picture)* appears after the volume and page number or numbers.

D

specific subject entry

general subject entry

subentry

identifier

cross-reference to preferred heading

cross-reference to additional heading

references listed in volume order

d (letter), rhyme about, 1/55

daddy longlegs, 4/137

dahlia, 4/8 (picture)

Daimler, Gottlieb (inventor), 9/53

daisy, 5/160 (with picture)

dam, 6/95

  energy from, 8/81

  of beaver, 4/41 (with picture)

Damascus (Syria), 14/93 (picture)

dance, 3/178-183 (with pictures)

  American Indian, 14/109 (picture),
    14/130 (with picture)

  Scottish, 14/115 (with picture)

  stories about

    Cinderella, 2/60-73

    Compae Rabbit's Ride, 2/124-129

dandelion, 5/23 (picture), 5/119
  (picture), 5/162 (with picture)

dark nebula, 7/120 (with picture)

date (fruit), 5/94 (with picture)

date bar (food), 12/76-77 (with
  pictures)

da Vinci, Leonardo, see Leonardo
  da Vinci

dawdling, by child, 15/55

day and night, 6/11

  on Earth, 7/18-19 (with pictures),
    7/72

  on Jupiter, 7/80

  on Mars, 7/74

  on Mercury, 7/67

  on moon, 7/57

  on Neptune, 7/87

  on Pluto, 7/88

  on Saturn, 7/82

  on Uranus, 7/84

  on Venus, 7/71

  see also night, poems about

day care, 15/91-93 (with picture)

Daylight Savings Time (McGinley),
  1/83

Day-of-the-Dead festival, 14/162-
  163 (with pictures)

days of the week, poems about

  Monday's Child, 1/77

  Solomon Grundy, 1/76

  Wash on Monday, 1/76

Dead Sea (Asia), 6/61 (with picture)

deafness, 11/78-79 (with pictures),
  12/138

volume number (in dark type) and page number reference to text only

reference to picture(s) only

volume 15 references are for parents and teachers

reference to both text and picture(s)

A

B

C

c (letter), rhyme about, 1/55
Cabana, Robert D. (astronaut),
7/181 *(picture)*
cabbage, 5/99 *(picture)*, 12/53
caber-throwing contest, 14/115
(with picture)
cable-stayed bridge, 9/162 *(with
pictures)*
cable television, 9/89 *(with
picture)*
cactus, 5/13 *(picture)*, 5/78-79 *(with
pictures)*, 5/127 *(picture)*, 5/170
barrel, 5/78
candelabra, 5/79 *(picture)*
pincushion, 5/79 *(pictures)*
prickly pear, 5/131 *(picture)*
saguaro, 5/34 *(picture)*
CAD, *see* **computer-aided
design**
caecilian, 4/89 *(with picture)*
Caesar, Julius (Roman emperor),
14/111 *(with picture)*
calcium, in diet, 11/159
calculator (machine), 8/179, 9/35
(with picture), 10/109 *(picture)*,
10/123-125 *(with pictures)*
see also **abacus**
calendar, 14/14-19 *(with pictures)*
April Fool's Day and, 14/74
as learning tool, 15/72
Chinese, 14/17 *(with picture)*,
14/42, 14/101, 14/145
Christian, 14/18
Hebrew, 14/18, 14/103, 14/141,
14/177
Islamic, 14/19, 14/30
Stonehenge as, 10/29
California, 6/29, 6/165 *(with
picture)*
caller ID, 9/101 *(with picture)*
Cambodia, 13/124
camel, 4/17 *(picture)*, 12/24
(picture), 12/34 *(picture)*, 12/51,
12/143 *(picture)*, 13/48-49 *(with
picture)*
camellia, 5/160
camera, 8/126-127 *(with pictures)*
digital, 9/11 *(picture)*
television, 9/88-89
Cameron, Ann (author)
Pudding Like a Night on the Sea, The,
2/166-177

camouflage, 4/148-149 *(with
pictures)*
Canada, 12/129 *(picture)*, 12/178,
13/16, 14/45, 14/86, 14/94,
14/115
ice hockey in, 12/91
sleds in, 13/42 *(with picture)*
special days in
Canada Day, 14/114 *(with
picture)*
Christmas, 14/180
Father's Day, 14/104-105
Remembrance Day, 14/166 *(with
pictures)*
Thanksgiving, 14/168, 14/169
Victoria Day, 14/92
see also **Inuit**
Canada Day, 14/114 *(with picture)*
canal, 13/100-101 *(with pictures)*
Cancer (constellation), 7/110 *(with
picture)*
candle, 12/24 *(picture)*, 12/26 *(with
pictures)*
burning of, 8/72 *(with picture)*
Cannon, Annie Jump
(astronomer), 7/157 *(with
picture)*
cannonball tree, 5/75 *(picture)*
canoe, 13/45
can opener, 9/148 *(picture)*
Canopus (star), 7/116
canopy (forest), 5/74-75 *(with
picture)*
cantilever bridge, 9/162 *(with
picture)*
canyon, 6/61 *(picture)*
Canyon de Chelly (Arizona), 6/61
(picture)
Cape Town (South Africa), 13/15
car, 13/40-41 *(with pictures)*
designing, 9/82-83 *(with pictures)*
gears in, 8/24-25
inertia and, 8/30-31
parts of, 9/54-55 *(with pictures)*
road signs, 12/143-145 *(with
pictures)*
robot in manufacturing, 9/174-175
(with picture)
toy, 12/102 *(picture)*
traveling by, with children, 15/98-
99 *(with picture)*
caravan, 13/49 *(with picture)*
carbohydrate, 11/158, 11/159
carbon, in telephone, 9/100 *(with
picture)*

carbon dioxide, 4/18, 5/112 *(with
picture)*, 6/169
in air, 7/73
in bread, 9/119
carbon monoxide detector,
15/61
careers
animal-related, 4/182-183 *(with
pictures)*
conservation, 6/179-181 *(with
pictures)*
construction, 9/156-157 *(with
picture)*
earth study, 6/42-45 *(with pictures)*,
6/59
engineering, see **engineer**
manufacturing, 9/146-147 *(with
pictures)*
mapmaking, 13/158-159 *(with
pictures)*
ocean study, 6/100-101 *(with
pictures)*
physical science, 8/180-183 *(with
pictures)*
plant-related, 5/120-123 *(with
pictures)*
space, 7/172-173 *(with picture)*
travel-related, 13/178-183 *(with
pictures)*
weather study, 6/146-147 *(with
pictures)*
caribou, 4/160-161 *(with picture)*,
12/62 *(picture)*
Caring (Madkour), 3/52-53 *(with
picture)*
Carle, Eric (artist), 3/18-19 *(with
pictures)*
carnivore, 4/13
carol (song), 14/179
carp, 3/11, 4/96 *(with picture)*,
14/88-91 *(with pictures)*
carpenter, 9/156 *(with picture)*
carpet, 12/38 *(picture)*, 12/126
(with picture)
carpool, 6/178, 13/41
Carroll, Lewis (author)
Jabberwocky, 1/152
Through the Looking Glass, 5/144-
149 *(with pictures)*
carrot, 5/97 *(with picture)*, 5/99
(picture), 5/138 *(picture)*, 12/53
cartilage, 11/102
cartographer, 13/159 *(with
picture)*
cartoon, 12/135 *(picture)*

D

d (letter), rhyme about, 1/55
daddy longlegs, 4/137
dahlia, 4/8 (picture)
Dai, 5/107 (with picture)
Daimler, Gottlieb (inventor), 9/53
daisy, 5/160 (with picture)
dam, 6/95
  energy from, 8/81
  of beaver, 4/41 (with picture)
Damascus (Syria), 14/93 (picture)
dance, 3/178-183 (with pictures)
  American Indian, 14/109 (picture),
    14/130 (with picture)
  Scottish, 14/115 (with picture)
  stories about
    Cinderella, 2/60-73
    Compae Rabbit's Ride, 2/124-129
dandelion, 5/23 (picture), 5/119
  (picture), 5/162 (with picture)
dark nebula, 7/120 (with picture)
date (fruit), 5/94 (with picture)
date bar (food), 12/76-77 (with
  pictures)
da Vinci, Leonardo, see
  Leonardo da Vinci
dawdling, by child, 15/55
day and night, 6/11
  on Earth, 7/18-19 (with pictures),
    7/72
  on Jupiter, 7/80
  on Mars, 7/74
  on Mercury, 7/67
  on moon, 7/57
  on Neptune, 7/87
  on Pluto, 7/88
  on Saturn, 7/82
  on Uranus, 7/84
  on Venus, 7/71
  see also night, poems about
day care, 15/91-93 (with picture)
Daylight Savings Time (McGinley),
  1/83
Day-of-the-Dead festival,
  14/162-163 (with pictures)
days of the week, poems about
  Monday's Child, 1/77
  Solomon Grundy, 1/76
  Wash on Monday, 1/76
Dead Sea (Asia), 6/61 (with picture)
deafness, 11/78-79 (with pictures),
  12/138

death, 11/140-141 (with pictures)
  explaining to child, 15/102-103
    (with picture)
decagon (shape), 10/37 (picture)
December, 14/170-181 (with
  pictures)
  birthdays in, 14/172-173 (with
    pictures)
  birthstone for, 6/33 (picture)
decibel, 8/157
decomposer, in food chain,
  4/163
deer, 4/155, 4/179
Degas, Edgar (artist), 3/60
degree (distance), 13/153
Deimos (moon), 7/60, 7/75
deinotherium (extinct animal),
  4/172-173 (with picture)
de la Mare, Walter (poet)
  Somewhere, 13/177
Delhi (India), 13/13
della Porta, Gianbattista
  (mathematician), 10/149
delphinium (plant), 5/142 (picture)
delta, 6/86 (with picture)
Delta rocket, 9/78 (picture)
Denmark, 6/178, 14/106
  story from
    Emperor's New Clothes, The, 2/36-
      47
dentist, 11/174-175 (with picture),
  15/59
Denver (Colorado), 6/63 (picture)
depth, of shape, 10/42 (with
  picture)
Derrah (game), 12/106-107 (with
  pictures)
desert, 4/70-71 (with pictures),
  6/64-67 (with pictures), 6/99,
  6/154 (picture)
  clothing for, 13/74-75 (with picture)
  plants of, 5/41 (with picture), 5/76-
    79 (with pictures)
  travel in, 13/48-49 (with picture)
design, 9/150 (with picture)
  see also computer-aided
    design; engineer
desk clerk, 13/178-179 (with
  picture)
dessert, 12/58-59 (with pictures)
development, of land, 6/166 (with
  picture)
Devil's Postpile (California), 6/29
diameter, of circle, 10/27 (with
  picture)

diamond (gem), 6/32-33 (with
  pictures)
Diana (goddess), 7/42
diaphragm (part of body), 11/51
  (with picture)
diaphragm (telephone), 9/100-101
  (with picture)
dice, 10/42 (picture), 10/110 (with
  picture)
  chance in rolling, 10/134-135 (with
    picture)
Dickson, Earle (inventor), 9/12
Diddle, Diddle, Dumpling (Mother
  Goose), 1/43
diet, see food
differences, individual, see
  uniqueness; sex differences
digestion, by plant, 5/48-49
digital camera, 9/11 (picture)
digital code, 9/30-31, 9/36-39
  (with picture), 9/106
digitalis, 5/117
digital thermometer, 9/14-15
  (with picture)
digital video disc, 9/40 (with
  picture)
Diller, a Dollar, A (Mother Goose),
  1/81
Dimetrodon (ancient lizardlike
  animal), 6/37 (picture)
dinosaur, 4/168-170 (with pictures),
  6/36 (with picture)
Dinosaur National Monument
  (Colorado), 13/109 (with picture)
directions
  on compass, 13/146
  on map, 13/136-137 (with picture)
director (theater), 3/152-153
disability
  learning, 15/109-111 (with picture)
  physical, 9/177 (with picture),
    11/130-131 (with picture),
    15/115-116 (with picture)
disabled, see disability
discipline, for children, 15/56-58
  (with picture), 15/113-115
disease, see illness
distance, on map, 13/140-141
  (with picture)
Divali (festival), 14/154-155 (with
  pictures)
division, 10/126-129 (with pictures)
division facts, 10/129
doctor, 11/153-155 (with pictures)
Doctor Foster Went to Gloucester
  (Mother Goose), 1/36

138

F

f (letter), rhyme about, 1/56
fables, 1/169
  Ant and the Dove, The, 1/174
  Blind Men and the Elephant, The,
    11/30-35 *(with pictures)*
  Crow and the Jug, The, 1/172
  Dog and the Bone, The, 1/175
  Hare and the Tortoise, The, 1/173
  How Chameleon Became a Teacher,
    1/176-181
  Lion and the Mouse, The, 1/171
fabric, 9/134-135 *(with pictures),*
  9/144-145 *(with pictures)*
  in crafts, 3/24-31 *(with pictures)*
face, 11/10-11 *(with pictures)*
  bones of, 11/40 *(with picture)*
  two sides of, 11/12-13 *(with*
    pictures)
factory
  assembly line in, 9/83 *(with*
    pictures), 9/146 *(with pictures)*
  workers in, 9/146-147 *(with*
    pictures)
Fahrenheit (temperature), 9/15
failure, in school, 15/79-80
fairy, see **elves and fairies,**
  stories about
fairy tales, 2/11
  Cinderella, 2/60-73
  Emperor's New Clothes, The, 2/36-
    47
  Jack and the Beanstalk, 2/12-21
  Old Woman and Her Dumpling, The,
    2/48-57
  Prince and the Orphan, The,
    2/74-87
  Shoemaker and the Elves, The,
    2/24-33
falcon, peregrine, 4/11, 4/59 *(with*
  picture)
fall (season), 5/56 *(with picture),*
  7/22-25 *(with picture)*
falls, poems about
  Humpty Dumpty, 1/22
  Ring-a-Ring o' Roses, 1/139
family, 12/9-13 *(with pictures)*
  activities, 12/20-25 *(with*
    pictures)
  drawing members of (project),
    11/131 *(with picture)*
  members looking alike, 11/100-
    101 *(with picture)*
  mental retardation and, 15/114

names, 12/14-17 *(with pictures)*
poems about
  My Little Golden Sister, 1/16
  Peter, Peter, Pumpkin-Eater, 1/25
  Rock-a-Bye Baby, 1/40
  Two Little Sisters, 1/17
  Walking, 1/16
problems in, 15/80
stories about
  Cinderella, 2/60-73
  Jack and the Beanstalk, 2/12-21
  Mother, Mother, I Want Another,
    2/140-147
  Pudding Like a Night on the Sea,
    The, 2/166-177
  Thousand Pails of Water, A, 2/181-
    189
traditions, 12/22-25 *(with pictures)*
types of, 11/108-109 *(with*
  pictures)
work sharing in, 12/166-167 *(with*
  pictures)
family day care, 15/92
family tree, 11/111-113 *(with*
  picture)
fan (machine), 9/11 *(picture),* 9/42
  (picture)
  hairdryer, 9/25 *(with picture)*
  vacuum cleaner, 9/23 *(with picture)*
Farjeon, Eleanor (poet)
  Kitten, A, 1/118
  Moon-Come-Out, 1/40
farmer, 4/183
farming, 13/78 *(with picture)*
far-sightedness, 11/73 *(with*
  picture)
fasting, 14/12, 14/30-31, 14/51,
  14/54, 14/75
fat, in diet, 11/158, 11/160,
  11/162-163 *(picture),* 11/169
father, 11/108, 12/10, 12/12,
  14/104-105 *(with picture)*
  baby's birth and, 11/92
  family tree and, 11/111 *(with*
    picture)
  genes from, 11/100-101 *(with*
    pictures)
  growing child and, 11/116-117
  see also **parent**
Father Christmas, 14/180,
  14/181
Father's Day, 14/104-105 *(with*
  picture)
fault-block mountain, 6/53 *(with*
  picture)
fax machine, 9/98 *(with picture)*

fear
  in preschooler, 15/55-56
  of death, 15/103
  unrealistic, 15/105-106, 15/108
feather, 4/50, 4/56-57 *(with*
  pictures)
February, 14/38-55 *(with pictures)*
  birthdays in, 14/40-41 *(with*
    pictures)
  birthstone for, 6/33 *(picture)*
feelings, see **thoughts and**
  feelings
feet, see **foot**
fern, 5/15 *(with picture),* 5/153 *(with*
  picture)
  ostrich plume, 4/8 *(picture)*
Ferris wheel, 10/26 *(with picture)*
ferry, 13/45
fiber, 5/108
  natural, 9/134-135 *(with pictures),*
    9/145 *(picture)*
  synthetic, 9/144-145 *(with pictures)*
fiberglass, 9/83, 9/163
fiber-optic cable, 8/136-137 *(with*
  picture)
Field, Rachel (poet)
  If Once You Have Slept on an Island,
    1/86
figurehead (carving), 3/10 *(with*
  picture)
Fiji, 12/21 *(picture),* 12/136 *(picture)*
filament, 8/166-167 *(with pictures)*
film (camera), 8/127 *(with picture)*
finger, 11/22
  bones of, 11/40 *(with picture),*
    11/42 *(picture)*
  touch, sense of, 11/87
fingernail, 11/24-25 *(with picture)*
finger painting, 3/43, 3/65 *(with*
  picture)
fingerprint, 11/26-27 *(with*
  pictures), 11/97, 11/120-121
finger spelling, 11/79 *(with picture)*
Finland, 13/43, 14/107
  music in, 3/117 *(picture)*
fins, 4/90
fir, Douglas, 5/38 *(picture)*
fire
  energy from, 8/72-73 *(with*
    pictures), 8/131 *(picture)*
  first use of (story), 8/104-111
    (with pictures)
  forest, 5/176-177 *(with pictures)*
  grassland, 5/60
Fire Bringer, The (story), 8/104-111
  (with pictures)
fire drill, 15/60

149

H

h (letter), rhyme about, 1/56
habitat, 4/56, 4/148, 4/166, 6/177
  people and, 4/174-175 *(with pictures)*
  plant, 5/171
haddock, 4/100
Hagia Sophia (church, Turkey), 13/123 *(with picture)*
haiku (poem), 1/164-167
hail, 6/144-145 *(with pictures)*
hair, 11/12, 11/16-17 *(with pictures)*, 11/19 *(picture)*, 11/120-121 *(with picture)*
hairdryer, 9/24-25 *(with pictures)*
hairstyle, 12/32 *(picture)*
hajj (journey), 14/93
Hale, Sara Josepha (poet)
  Mary Had a Little Lamb, 1/14
Hale telescope, 7/157 *(picture)*
halite (mineral), 6/27
Halley, Edmund (astronomer), 7/106
Halley's Comet, 7/106-107 *(with pictures)*
Halloween, 14/156 *(with picture)*
Ham (chimpanzee), 7/164
hammer, 3/93 *(picture)*
hamster, 4/27 *(picture)*, 4/29 *(with picture)*
hand, 11/13, 11/22-23 *(with pictures)*, 11/26 *(picture)*
  as measurement, 10/160-161 *(with picture)*
  bones in, 11/42 *(picture)*
  eating with, 12/66-67 *(with picture)*
  game with, 12/88-89 *(with pictures)*
  multiplication using, 10/117 *(with pictures)*
  washing, 11/178-179
  see also finger
hand puppet, 3/166-167 *(with picture)*
Hanukkah, 14/176-177 *(with pictures)*
happiness, 11/122-125 *(with picture)*, 11/141
  poem about, 1/84
Happy Thought (Stevenson), 1/84
harbor, 13/46-47 *(with picture)*
hare, story about, 1/173
Hare and the Tortoise, The (Aesop), 1/173
harmony, 3/128, 3/129, 3/137

harp, 3/117 *(with picture)*
harpsichord, 3/122
harvest, 5/102 *(picture)*, 12/21 *(picture)*, 12/49 *(picture)*
harvest festivals, 14/10, 14/135
  Homowo, 14/132-133
  Kwanzaa, 14/182 *(with picture)*
  Mid-Autumn Festival, 14/145
  Thanksgiving, 14/168-169 *(with pictures)*
  Yule, 14/179
hat, for puppet (project), 3/172-173 *(with pictures)*
Hausa (people), 3/154
Hawaii, 6/69, 6/81 *(picture)*
  erosion in, 5/169
hawk, 5/60 *(with picture)*
Hawking, Stephen (scientist), 7/157 *(with picture)*
hazel, 5/58 *(picture)*
head, 4/126 *(picture)*
  human baby, 11/98, 11/99 *(with picture)*, 11/106 *(with picture)*
  see also brain; skull
head, of river, 6/85
headache, 11/153
headphones, 9/87 *(picture)*
heads or tails, *see* coin tossing, and chance
healing, 11/148-149 *(with pictures)*
health, 11/144-179 *(with pictures)*
  cleanliness for, 11/178-179
  doctor visits and, 11/154-156 *(with pictures)*
  eating for, 5/116-117 *(with pictures)*, 11/158-169 *(with pictures)*
  exercising for, 11/156, 11/170-171 *(with pictures)*
  of preschool child, 15/59-61 *(with picture)*
  of school-age child, 15/74-76
  of teeth, 11/172-175 *(with pictures)*
  pain and, 11/68-69, 11/152-153 *(with pictures)*
  sleep and, 11/176-177
hearing (sense), 11/60 *(with picture)*, 11/68-69 *(with picture)*, 11/76-77 *(with pictures)*
  problems with, 11/78-79 *(with pictures)*, 11/157 *(with picture)*
  see also ear
hearing aid, 11/78 *(with pictures)*
Hearn, Lafcadio (author)
  Old Woman and Her Dumpling, The, 2/48-57

heart, 11/43, 11/46-47 *(with pictures)*, 11/61 *(with picture)*
  exercising, 11/170-171
heartbeat, 11/155-156 *(with picture)*
heat, 8/87-111 *(with pictures)*
  electricity and, 8/168-169 *(with picture)*
  energy from, 8/73, 8/75, 8/84-85 *(with pictures)*
  hairdryer as source of, 9/24-25 *(with pictures)*
  hot-air balloon and, 8/96-97 *(with picture)*
  infrared rays and, 8/133
  light and, 8/114-115, 8/130 *(picture)*
  molecule motion and, 8/88-89 *(with pictures)*, 8/92-95 *(with pictures)*
  see also fire; temperature
heating duct, 9/154 *(picture)*
heaven and earth (food), 12/68
Hebrew (language), 12/131 *(picture)*, 13/30-31
Hebrew calendar, 14/18, 14/103, 14/141, 14/177
hedgehog, 4/147 *(with picture)*
height, 10/162 *(with picture)*
  human, 15/85-90 *(with pictures)*
height, human, 11/105 *(with picture)*, 11/154 *(with picture)*
Hekla, Mount (Iceland), 6/54 *(picture)*
helicopter, 9/12, 9/44 *(picture)*, 9/72-73 *(with pictures)*, 9/81 *(with picture)*, 13/55
  on ship, 9/69 *(with picture)*
  paper (project), 8/34-35 *(with pictures)*
Helios (god), 7/30
"hello," ways of saying, 12/130-131 *(with picture)*
helmet, 9/53 *(with pictures)*
helpers, stories about
  Cinderella, 2/60-73
  It's My Birthday, 2/148-157
  Little Red Hen, The, 2/90-92
  Pudding Like a Night on the Sea, The, 2/166-177
  Shoemaker and the Elves, The, 2/24-33
  Thousand Pails of Water, A, 2/181-189
hemispheres, of earth, 7/24, 7/114-117 *(with pictures)*, 13/150-151 *(with pictures)*
hemlock, 5/38

I

i (letter), rhyme about, 1/57
I Ate a Ton of Sugar (Gilbert),
1/28
ibex, Pyrenean, 4/179 *(picture)*
ice, 8/88 *(with picture)*
  crystals of, in clouds, 6/124-125
  in Antarctica, 13/20-21
  in glacier, 6/70-71 *(with picture)*
  poem about
    Ice, 1/83
  travel on, 13/42-43 *(with pictures)*
  see also **hail; snow**
Ice (Aldis), 1/83
iceberg, 6/71
ice cream, 9/124-125 *(with*
  pictures), 14/120 *(with pictures)*
Iceland, 6/69, 14/89
  volcanoes of, 6/54 *(picture)*, 6/56-
  57 *(with pictures)*
ichthyologist (scientist), 4/183
identical twins, 11/101 *(with*
  picture)
I Eat My Peas with Honey
  (poem), 1/33
If All the World Were Paper
  (Mother Goose), 1/32
If Once You Have Slept on an
  Island (Field), 1/86
igneous rock, 6/23 *(with picture)*
ignition, car, 9/56 *(with picture)*
Iguaçu Falls (South America),
  13/19, 13/117 *(with picture)*,
  13/162 *(picture)*
iguana, 4/69 *(picture)*
I Had a Little Hobby Horse
  (Mother Goose), 1/104
I Had a Little Pig (poem), 1/113
illness, 11/146-147
  height and, 15/90
  insects and, 4/130-131 *(with*
    pictures)
  lack of sleep and, 11/177
  of school-age child, 15/75-76
  pain and, 11/152-153 *(with*
    pictures)
  see also **injury** *and specific illnesses*
I Love You, I Love You (poem),
  1/15
imagination, in preschoolers,
  15/52-53
I Met a Man (poem), 1/24
immunization, 11/157, 15/74

impressionism, 3/48 *(with picture)*,
  3/54-55 *(with pictures)*, 3/60-61 *(with*
  pictures), 3/67
Inca (people), 13/104
incense, 14/117
inch, 10/163
inch-pound system, 10/163
inclined plane, 8/14-15 *(with*
  picture), 8/19
Independence Day
  Bolívar's birthday, 14/121 *(with*
    picture)
  in Brazil, 14/139 *(with picture)*
  in Equatorial Guinea, 14/69
  in Greece, 14/69 *(with picture)*
  in India, 14/35
  in Indonesia, 14/129
  in Mauritius, 14/69
  in Mexico, 14/142-143 *(with*
    picture)
  in United States, 14/116 *(with*
    picture)
India, 12/24, 12/31 *(picture)*, 12/33
  (picture), 12/99, 12/178, 13/95
  (picture), 13/100
  arts of
    dance, 3/179 *(picture)*, 3/182-183
      (with pictures)
    kites, 12/104
    music, 3/125 *(with picture)*, 3/127
      (with picture)
    theater, 3/147 *(with picture)*
  clothing in, 13/74 *(picture)*
  food in, 12/39 *(picture)*, 12/47,
    12/50
  forest in, 5/159 *(picture)*
  funeral in, 12/25
  games in, 12/81 *(picture)*, 12/86
    (with picture)
  Ganges River in, 13/125 *(with*
    picture)
  language of, 12/131 *(picture)*
  proverb from, 1/183
  school in, 12/115 *(picture)*, 12/118
    (picture), 12/124 *(picture)*
  special days in
    Buddha's birthday, 14/75
    Divali, 14/154-155 *(with pictures)*
    Gandhi's birthday, 14/151 *(with*
      picture)
    New Year, 14/26
  star myth from, 7/112 *(with*
    picture), 7/141
  stories from
    Blind Men and the Elephant, The,
      11/30-35

How the Turtle Saved His Own Life,
  2/93-95
  transportation in, 13/37 *(with*
    picture)
  see also **Taj Mahal**
Indian Ocean, 6/74 *(with picture)*
Indian pipe plant, 5/13 *(with*
  picture)
Indians, American, 14/109
  (picture), 14/169 *(with picture)*
  ceremonies of, 12/26
  clothing of, 12/28 *(picture)*
  corn legend of, 5/92-93 *(with*
    pictures)
  dances, 3/178 *(with picture)*
  moon myth of, 7/43-44 *(with*
    picture)
  poems of
    Away in the East, 1/46
    By the Sandy Water, 1/85
    This Land, 1/86
  sign language of, 12/139 *(with*
    pictures)
  sky myth of, 7/141 *(with picture)*
  song of, 1/40
  story from
    Glooscap and His People, 2/130-
      137
  sun myth of, 7/28-29 *(with picture)*
  totem poles of, 3/94-95 *(with*
    pictures)
  tribal name of, 12/26
  weaving by, 12/38 *(picture)*
  see also **Inuit** *and specific tribes*
Indonesia, 12/53, 12/59 *(picture)*
  game from, 12/89 *(with picture)*
  Independence Day in, 14/129 *(with*
    picture)
  music in, 3/111 *(with picture)*
industry, and pollution, 6/177
  (with picture)
inertia, 8/30-31 *(with pictures)*
infant, *see* **baby**
infinite number, 10/107
influenza, *see* **flu**
information, and brain, 11/62-63
  (with picture)
infrared rays, 8/133, 9/15, 9/31,
  9/93
ingot, 9/139
injector, in car, 9/57 *(with picture)*
injury
  healing, 11/148-149 *(with pictures)*
  pain and, 11/152-153 *(with*
    pictures)
  types of, 11/150-151 *(with*
    pictures)

J

K

k (letter), rhyme about, 1/57

Kaaba (building, Saudi Arabia), 13/124-125

Kabuki (theater), 3/149 (with picture)

Kalahari Desert (Africa), 7/28, 12/112 (picture)

Kalundborg (Denmark), 6/178

kangaroo, 4/10 (picture), 4/36-37 (with pictures)

kantele (musical instrument), 3/117 (picture)

karamu (ceremony), 14/182 (picture)

Keller, Irene (poet)
Thingumajigs, 1/90-91

kelp, 5/52 (picture)

Kennedy Space Center (Florida), 7/179 (picture), 7/181 (picture)

Kenya, 12/28 (picture), 12/32-33, 13/65, 13/119 (with picture)

Kepler, Johannes (scientist), 7/143

keratin (skin), 11/24

kerigami (craft), 3/22-23 (with pictures)

kettle drum, 3/115

key, 9/149 (picture)

keyboard, 9/35 (picture)

keyboard instrument, 3/122 (with picture)

keystone, 9/161 (with picture)

Keystone Canyon (Alaska), 13/39 (picture)

Khafre (king of Egypt), 3/90

Khufu (king of Egypt), 3/90

kibbutz (community), 12/11 (with picture)

kidney, 11/56-57 (with pictures)

Kilimanjaro (mountain, Africa), 13/15

kiln, 9/133

kilometer (measurement), 10/163

kilt, 14/115 (with picture)

kilt (clothing), 12/29 (picture)

kimono (clothing), 12/24 (picture), 12/30 (picture), 14/164 (picture)

kinara (candleholder), 14/182 (with picture)

kindergarten, 15/70, 15/77-78

king, 12/14, 12/179 (picture)
poems about
Humpty Dumpty, 1/22
Old King Cole, 1/20
Sing a Song of Sixpence, 1/28
stories about
Emperor's New Clothes, The, 2/36-47
Prince and the Orphan, The, 2/74-87

King, Martin Luther, Jr. (civil rights leader), 14/36-37 (with pictures)

kingdom, 5/11

kingfisher (bird), 4/52 (picture)

kite, 3/11 (with picture), 8/67 (with picture), 8/68 (with picture), 12/79, 12/104 (with picture), 14/90-91 (with pictures)

Kitten, A (Farjeon), 1/118

kneecap, 11/40 (with picture)

knee pad (equipment), 11/183

knife, 3/95 (picture), 8/16 (with picture)

koala, 4/36, 4/37, 4/182 (picture)

kola nut, 5/104 (with picture)

Korea, 12/104, 14/42, 14/75, 14/145 (with picture)

Kosciuszko, Mount (Australia), 13/25

Krak des Chevaliers (castle, Syria), 13/89 (with picture)

Kremlin (Moscow), 13/95 (picture)

Krikalev, Sergei Konstantinovich (cosmonaut), 7/181 (picture)

Krishna (god), 14/63

Kuiper belt (comets), 7/104

kutyapi (musical instrument), 3/124 (with picture)

Kwanzaa, 14/182 (with picture)

L

l (letter), rhyme about, 1/58
laboratory, space, *see* space station
Labor Day, 14/65, 14/87 *(with picture)*
ladybug, 4/159 *(picture)*, 4/160
Lagos (Nigeria), 13/15
Laika (dog), 7/164 *(with picture)*
lake, 6/92-97 *(with pictures)*
Lake Baikal (Russia), 6/97 *(with picture)*
Lake Eyre (Australia), 6/94 *(picture)*
Lake Maracaibo (South America), 6/96-97 *(with picture)*
Lake Ndudu (Tanzania), 6/97 *(picture)*
Lake Superior (North America), 6/92
Lake Tanganyika (Africa), 13/14-15
Lake Titicaca (South America), 13/44 *(picture)*
Lake Victoria (Africa), 6/97
Lake Winnipeg (Canada), 6/96
Lakshmi (goddess), 14/155 *(with picture)*
lamb, *see* sheep
lammergeier, African (bird), 4/12 *(picture)*
LAN (network), 9/106 *(picture)*
land, 6/46 *(with picture)*
  clearing of, 5/170-171 *(with picture)*
landscape architect, 5/122
landscaper, 9/157 *(with picture)*
language, 12/128-133 *(with pictures)*, 13/30-31
  preschool development of, 15/49
Lanterns, Festival of, 14/117 *(with picture)*
Lao (people), 12/23
Lapland, 12/50 *(with picture)*
Lapps (people), 13/43 *(with picture)*
larynx, 3/113 *(picture)*, 11/74
La Scala (theater), 3/150-151 *(with picture)*
Lascaux (France), 3/41 *(picture)*
laser, 8/134-135 *(with picture)*
  in compact disc player, 9/30 *(with picture)*, 9/41 *(with picture)*
  in hologram, 9/32-33 *(with pictures)*
  in phone system, 9/99

laser printer, 9/39 *(with picture)*
latex, 5/108 *(with pictures)*
latitude, 13/152-153 *(with picture)*
launches
  rocket, 7/158-161
  space shuttle, 7/170-171 *(with pictures)*, 7/178-181 *(with pictures)*
lava, 6/42 *(with picture)*, 6/54-55 *(with picture)*, 8/130 *(picture)*
law, 12/164-165 *(with pictures)*
lawn mower, 9/42 *(picture)*
leader, 12/173
  of government, 12/178-179 *(with pictures)*
  stories about
    Emperor's New Clothes, The, 2/36-47
    Glooscap and His People, 2/130-137
    Prince and the Orphan, The, 2/74-87
leaf, 5/16-17 *(with picture)*, 5/21 *(with pictures)*
  Amazonian water lily, 5/66-67
  as food, 5/96-97 *(with pictures)*
  color of, 5/18-19 *(with pictures)*, 5/56
  deciduous tree, 5/36-37 *(with pictures)*, 5/56
  needleleaf, 5/38-39 *(with pictures)*
  pollution damage to, 5/175 *(with picture)*
  pressed (project), 3/32-33 *(with picture)*
Lear, Edward (poet)
  limericks, 1/158, 1/160, 1/161
  Owl and the Pussycat, The, 1/130-131
learning, 12/111-127 *(with pictures)*
  about school, 11/119
  about the world, 11/116-117, 11/120-121
  by mentally retarded, 15/113
  etiquette, 12/154-155
  languages, 12/128
  right from wrong, 11/138-139 *(with pictures)*
  special skills, 12/126 *(with picture)*
  see also school; teacher
learning disability, 15/109-111 *(with picture)*
Le Corbusier (architect), 13/115
leek, 5/117
leg, artificial, 9/177 *(picture)*
leg bone, 11/41 *(picture)*, 11/42

legend (map), 13/136, 13/139 *(with picture)*
legends, *see* folk tales
lemming, 4/160-161, 5/80
lemonade, 12/70-71 *(with picture)*
length (measurement), 10/12, 10/158 *(with picture)*
  measuring (exercises), 10/164-165 *(with pictures)*, 10/172 *(with picture)*
  of shape, 10/42 *(with picture)*
lens, 8/122-123 *(with picture)*
  air as, 8/124
  camera, 8/126-127 *(with pictures)*
  telescope, 7/146 *(with picture)*
Lent, 14/51-55 *(with pictures)*
Leonardo da Vinci (inventor), 9/12 *(with picture)*
Leonov, Alexei A. (cosmonaut), 7/165
leopard, snow, 5/84 *(picture)*
lettuce, 5/96-97 *(with picture)*, 5/99 *(picture)*, 5/139 *(with picture)*, 12/52 *(picture)*
lever, 8/10-13 *(with pictures)*, 8/37
Lhote, Henri (explorer), 3/40
lice, head, 15/76
licorice, 5/104
life, 5/10-11
  and Mars, 7/76-77
  and moon, 7/41
lifting
  of airplane's wings in flight, 8/42-43 *(with pictures)*
  with inclined plane, 8/14-15 *(with picture)*
  with lever, 8/10-11 *(with picture)*
  with pulley, 8/22-23 *(with picture)*
  see also pulling; pushing
light, 8/112-137 *(with pictures)*
  bending by lens, 8/122-125 *(with pictures)*
  from burning, 8/73
  from stars, 7/100
  from sun, 7/14-17
  in painting, 3/56-57 *(with pictures)*
  laser, 8/134-135 *(with picture)*
  reflected, 8/116-117 *(with pictures)*, 8/120-121 *(with pictures)*
  speed of, 7/14
  through wires, 8/136-137 *(with picture)*
  see also color; shadow; sunlight
light bulb, 8/114, 8/166-167 *(with picture)*, 9/10 *(picture)*, 9/12 *(with picture)*

M

m (letter), rhyme about, 1/58
machine, **8**/8-27 *(with pictures)*
 friction and, **8**/32-37 *(with pictures)*
 steam-powered, **8**/99
 types of
  gear, **8**/24-25 *(with pictures)*
  inclined plane, **8**/14-15 *(with picture)*
  lever, **8**/10-13 *(with pictures)*, **8**/37
  pulley, **8**/22-23 *(with pictures)*
  screw, **8**/18-19 *(with pictures)*
  wedge, **8**/16-17 *(with pictures)*
  wheel and axle, **8**/20-21 *(with pictures)*
 see also **invention**
Machu Picchu (ruins, Peru), **13**/19, **13**/104 *(with picture)*
Ma'dan (people), **5**/107 *(with picture)*
Madkour, Nazli (artist), **3**/52-53 *(with pictures)*
Magellan, Ferdinand (explorer), **13**/156
Magellanic Clouds (galaxies), **7**/131 *(with picture)*
maggot, **12**/62 *(picture)*
magic, stories about
 Cinderella, **2**/60-73
 Glooscap and His People, **2**/130-137
 Jack and the Beanstalk, **2**/12-21
 Old Woman and Her Dumpling, The, **2**/48-57
 Shoemaker and the Elves, The, **2**/24-33
magic number, in name (exercise), **10**/96-97 *(with picture)*
magic square, **10**/92-95 *(with pictures)*
magma, **6**/29, **6**/54
magnet, **8**/38-39 *(with pictures)*, **15**/72 *(with picture)*
 compass as, **13**/146
 generator and, **8**/170
 superconducting, **8**/169
 see also **electromagnet**
magnetic poles, of earth, **7**/137, **13**/146-147
magnetic tape, **9**/28-29 *(with picture)*
magnet raft (project), **9**/66-67 *(with pictures)*

magnifying glass, **8**/123 *(with picture)*
Maia (goddess), **14**/83
makeup, **3**/162-163 *(with pictures)*, **3**/177 *(with pictures)*
Malawi (Africa), **12**/126, **14**/95
Malaysia, **13**/112 *(with picture)*, **14**/101
mallard, **4**/65 *(picture)*
mallet, **8**/17 *(with picture)*
Mama, Raouf (author)
 How Chameleon Became a Teacher (story), **1**/176-181
 Prince and the Orphan, The, **2**/74-87
mammal, **4**/24 *(with pictures)*, **4**/32-49 *(with pictures)*
 baby, **4**/14-15 *(with picture)*, **4**/34-35 *(with pictures)*
 largest/smallest, **4**/48-49 *(with pictures)*, **4**/144 *(with picture)*
 see also **animal,** habitat of
mammalogist (scientist), **4**/183
mammoth, **4**/173 *(with picture)*
manatee, **4**/47 *(with picture)*
Mancala (game), **12**/108-109 *(with pictures)*
mandarin (duck), **4**/65 *(picture)*
Mandarin Chinese (language), **13**/30-31
mangrove, **5**/66 *(with picture)*
manners, *see* **etiquette**
manta ray, **4**/25 *(picture)*, **4**/97
mantle, of earth, **6**/21, **6**/48 *(with picture)*
manufacturing, **9**/146-147 *(with pictures)*
Maori (people), **3**/10, **7**/30, **14**/44
map, **12**/127 *(picture)*, **13**/126-159 *(with pictures)*
 air-traffic control, **9**/95 *(picture)*
 CD-coded, **13**/41
 directions on, **13**/136-137 *(with picture)*
 distance measurement on, **13**/140-141 *(with picture)*
 early, **13**/156-157 *(with pictures)*
 equator on, **13**/150-151 *(with picture)*
 latitude and longitude on, **13**/152-153 *(with picture)*
 see also **globe**
maple sugar, **12**/58 *(picture)*
maple tree, **5**/59 *(with picture)*
Maracaibo, Lake (South America), **6**/96-97 *(with picture)*

marble (material), **3**/92-93 *(with picture)*, **6**/25 *(with picture)*
marbles (game), **12**/87 *(with picture)*
March, **14**/56-69 *(with pictures)*
 birthdays in, **14**/58-59 *(with pictures)*
 birthstone for, **6**/33 *(picture)*
Marconi, Guglielmo (inventor), **9**/86 *(with picture)*
Marcos, Ferdinand (Filipino leader), **14**/49
Mardi Gras, **14**/51-53 *(with pictures)*
margarine, **5**/95
marigold, **5**/14 *(picture)*, **5**/140 *(picture)*
 burr, **5**/23
marimba, **3**/110, **3**/115 *(with picture)*
marine biologist, **6**/101 *(with picture)*
Mariner 10 (spacecraft), **7**/68 *(with picture)*
marionette, **3**/167 *(with picture)*
marmot, alpine (animal), **5**/84
marriage, **12**/23-24 *(with pictures)*
marrow, **11**/43 *(with picture)*, **11**/48 *(picture)*
Mars (god), **14**/57 *(with picture)*
Mars (planet), **7**/65 *(picture)*, **7**/74-79 *(with pictures)*, **7**/97
 moons of, **7**/60, **7**/75
 origin of name, **7**/91 *(with picture)*
Mars Pathfinder (spacecraft), **7**/77 *(with picture)*
martial arts, **12**/90 *(picture)*
Martin Luther King, Jr., Day, **14**/36-37 *(with pictures)*
Mary, Mary, Quite Contrary (Mother Goose), **1**/22
Mary Had a Little Lamb (Hale), **1**/14
Mary Had a Pretty Bird (Mother Goose), **1**/95
Masai (people), **12**/33, **12**/57
mask, **3**/178 *(with picture)*
 snow leopard (project), **14**/76-77 *(with pictures)*
match, safety, **9**/148 *(picture)*
materials engineer, **9**/169 *(with picture)*
mathematics, *see* **measurement; number; shape**
mating, **4**/152-153 *(with pictures)*

N

P

p (letter), rhyme about, 1/59
Pacific Islands, 13/10
 folktale from
  Maui Tames the Sun, **7**/32-33 *(with picture)*
Pacific Ocean, 6/49, 6/69, 6/74 *(with pictures)*
pager, 9/102, 9/109 *(picture)*
pain, 11/61, 11/63, 11/68-69, 11/121, 11/152-153 *(with pictures)*
paint
 for art, **3**/42-47 *(with pictures)*
 grease, **3**/163
Painted Desert (Arizona), **6**/65 *(pictures)*
painter, 9/157 *(with picture)*
painting, 3/39-77 *(with pictures)*
 by Cassatt, **3**/60-61 *(with pictures)*
 by Madkour, **3**/52-53 *(with pictures)*
 by Morisot, **3**/54-55 *(with pictures)*
 color in, **3**/48-49 *(with pictures),* **3**/52-53 *(with pictures)*
 contrast in, **3**/56-57 *(with pictures)*
 detail in, **3**/54-55 *(with pictures),* **3**/67-68 *(with pictures)*
 perspective in, **3**/58-59 *(with pictures)*
 prehistoric, **3**/40-41 *(with pictures)*
paint roller, 9/42 *(picture)*
Paiute Indians, 8/104-111 *(with pictures)*
Pakistan, 12/57 *(with picture),* **12**/91 *(with picture),* **14**/63
paleontologist (scientist), **4**/183, **6**/45 *(with picture)*
palette (project), **3**/46-47 *(with pictures)*
palm tree, 5/35 *(picture),* **5**/170
pampas, 5/62 *(with picture)*
Panama, 14/121
Panama Canal, 13/100-101 *(with picture)*
Pancake Day, 14/52 *(with picture)*
panda, giant, 4/20 *(with picture),* **4**/179 *(picture),* **13**/121
pangolin (animal), **4**/146 *(with picture)*
panpipe (musical instrument), **3**/110
Papago Indians, 1/85
papel picado (craft), **3**/20 *(with pictures)*

paper, 5/111-112 *(with picture),* **9**/126-129 *(with pictures)*
"Paper, Scissors, Rock" (game), **12**/89
paper bag, 9/12
paper cutting (craft), **3**/20-21 *(with pictures)*
paper folding (craft), see **origami**
paper lantern (project), **3**/22-23 *(with picture)*
paper mat (project), **3**/30-31 *(with pictures)*
papier-mâché (craft), **3**/102-103 *(with pictures)*
Papua New Guinea, 10/71, 12/52 *(picture),* **12**/86 *(picture)*
papyrus, 5/66 *(with picture),* **13**/44
parachute, 9/12 *(with picture)*
parade, 12/170-171 *(with picture)*
 Bastille Day, **14**/118 *(picture)*
 Chinese New Year, **14**/42 *(with picture)*
 Day of the Dead, **14**/163 *(with picture)*
 Mardi Gras, **14**/53 *(picture)*
 Moomba, **14**/65 *(with picture)*
 New Year's Day, **14**/27 *(picture)*
 Republic Day (India), **14**/34-35 *(with picture)*
 St. Patrick's Day, **14**/61
 United Nations Day, **14**/157 *(picture)*
parakeet, 4/29 *(picture)*
parallelogram (shape), **10**/33 *(with picture),* **10**/36 *(picture)*
paramecium, 4/117 *(with picture)*
parent, 11/108, 12/10-12 *(with pictures),* **14**/104-105 *(picture)*
 as role model, **15**/65-66
 baby's birth and, **11**/92
 concerns of
  day care, choice of, **15**/91-93
  death, feelings about, **15**/102-103
  growth of child, **15**/85-90
  health and safety, **15**/59-61, **15**/74-76, **15**/100-101
  Internet, influence of, **15**/95
  moving, **15**/96-97
  problem behavior, **15**/55-58, **15**/77-81, **15**/104-108
  television, influence of, **15**/53-54, **15**/60, **15**/66, **15**/94-95
  travel, **15**/98-99
 family tree and, **11**/111 *(with picture)*

 genes from, **11**/100-101 *(with pictures)*
 growing child and, **11**/116-117
 of disabled child, **15**/115-116
 of learning disabled child, **15**/110-111
 of mentally-retarded child, **15**/112-114
 of preschool child, **15**/48-63
 of school-age child, **15**/64-83
 resources for, **15**/117
 teacher conferences with, **15**/73 *(with picture),* **15**/79
 see also **father; mother**
parental control software, 15/95
parent-cooperative school, 15/54
parent-education program, 15/116
Paris (France), **14**/119 *(with picture)*
 Eiffel Tower in, **13**/97 *(with picture)*
 Louvre in, **13**/114-115 *(with picture)*
 theater in, **3**/146
Paris-Auteuil (Utrillo), **3**/59 *(with picture)*
park, 6/159 *(picture),* **6**/167 *(picture),* **6**/182 *(picture)*
parka, 13/73 *(with picture)*
Parliament, Houses of (London), **13**/95 *(picture)*
Parliament House (New Delhi, India), **13**/95 *(picture)*
parrot, 4/16, 4/25 *(picture),* **4**/60 *(with picture),* **5**/72 *(with picture)*
 imperial, **4**/178 *(picture)*
parsley, 5/99 *(picture),* **5**/136 *(picture),* **5**/137 *(picture)*
Parthenon (Greece), **13**/107 *(with picture)*
passenger train, 9/60-61 *(with picture)*
passion-flower, 5/13 *(picture),* **5**/74 *(picture)*
Passover, 14/80-81 *(with pictures)*
Pat-a-Cake (Mother Goose), **1**/137
patchwork quilt, 3/24-25 *(with picture)*
patent, 9/13
Paterson, "Banjo" (composer), **3**/139
Patience (poem), **1**/89
Patrick, St. (Irish saint), **14**/61

Q

R

r (letter), rhyme about, 1/60
rabbit, 4/155 *(picture),* 4/162 *(with picture),* 5/56 *(picture),* 5/168-169
  in art, 3/71-73 *(with pictures)*
  poems about
    Here Is a Bunny, 1/136
    Rabbit, The, 1/107
  stories about
    Compae Rabbit's Ride, 2/124-129
    Hare and the Tortoise, The, 1/173
Rabbit, The (Roberts), 1/107
raccoon, 4/13 *(picture)*
radar, 9/94-95, 9/97
  Doppler, 6/147
radiation
  from space, 7/134-135 *(with picture)*
  on Jupiter, 7/81
radio, 9/10 *(picture),* 9/86 *(with pictures)*
radio-controlled car (toy), 9/93, 9/109 *(picture)*
radiosonde (instrument), 6/147
radio transmitter, 9/86, 9/97, 9/102-103
radio wave
  in radio, 9/86
  in remote control, 9/93
  in telephone system, 9/99, 9/102-103
  in television, 9/89
  satellite as transmitter of, 9/104-105 *(with picture)*
  see also **radar**
radish, 5/97 *(with picture),* 5/99 *(picture),* 5/138 *(with picture),* 12/52 *(picture)*
radium, 8/56-57 *(with pictures)*
radius, of circle, 10/27 *(with picture)*
rafflesia, 5/167 *(with picture)*
railroad, *see* **train**
rain, 6/134-141 *(with pictures)*
  acid, *see* **acid rain**
  desert, 6/65
  flooding from, 6/90-91 *(with pictures)*
  hail and, 6/144-145
  hurricane, 6/120, 6/121
  poems about
    Doctor Foster Went to Gloucester, 1/36

    Rain, Rain, 1/36
    Rain on the Green Grass, 1/37
  rainbow and, 6/138-139
Rain, Rain (Mother Goose), 1/36
rainbow, 6/138-139 *(with pictures),* 8/132-133
rain forest, tropical, 4/175, 5/72-75 *(with pictures),* 13/19, 13/117
  destruction of, 5/172-173 *(with pictures),* 6/176-177 *(with picture)*
rain gauge (project), 6/136-137 *(with pictures)*
Rain on the Green Grass (Mother Goose), 1/37
Ramadan, 14/30-31 *(with pictures)*
Ramírez de Arellano, Rafael (author)
  Compae Rabbit's Ride, 2/124-129
ramp, 8/15
Ramphorhynchus (extinct reptile), 4/168 *(picture)*
rancher, 4/183
ranger, 4/183
rapid (river), 6/85 *(with picture)*
rat
  kangaroo, 4/41 *(picture)*
  poem about
    Three Young Rats, 1/113
raw materials, 9/110 *(with picture)*
Re (god), 7/30 *(with picture)*
reading
  about places, 13/62, 13/64-69, 13/169
  to preschoolers, 15/19, 15/51-52 *(with picture)*
  to school-age child, 15/72, 15/83
Reason, The (Aldis), 1/129
reasoning, with child, 15/57-58
recipes, 12/70-77 *(with pictures)*
  breakfast sundae, 11/164-165 *(with pictures)*
  bruschetta, 12/72-73 *(with pictures)*
  crunchies, 5/104 *(with picture)*
  date bars, 12/76-77 *(with pictures)*
  fufu, 12/74-75 *(with pictures)*
  ice cream, 9/124-125 *(with pictures),* 14/120 *(with pictures)*
  lemonade, 12/70-71 *(with picture)*
  pizza, 11/167 *(with pictures)*
  punch, 14/28
  rice cakes, 14/50 *(with picture)*
  salad, 5/98-101 *(with pictures)*
  snack kabob, 11/166 *(with pictures)*
  sweet apple slices, 14/141 *(with picture)*

recreation, *see* **game; sports**
rectangle (shape), 10/9-11 *(with pictures),* 10/36 *(picture)*
  making from squares (exercise), 10/25 *(with picture)*
  tangram (exercise), 10/32-33 *(with pictures)*
rectum, 11/55 *(with picture)*
recumbent bicycle, 9/51 *(with picture)*
recycling
  paper, 9/127-129 *(with pictures)*
  rain, 6/134-135 *(with pictures)*
  resources, 5/111, 5/182, 6/163, 6/175 *(with picture),* 6/182-183 *(with pictures)*
red (color), 6/106-107, 8/128, 8/131, 8/133, 9/89-90
red blood cell, 11/48 *(picture),* 11/49 *(picture)*
Red Bottle (Cragg), 3/100 *(picture)*
redwood, 5/38 *(with picture)*
reed (plant), 5/107 *(with pictures)*
reef, coral, *see* **coral reef**
reflection
  light, 7/46-47 *(with pictures),* 7/64, 8/116-117 *(with pictures),* 8/120-121 *(with pictures),* 8/128, 8/129
  sound, 8/152-155
reflective nebula, 7/120 *(with picture)*
refrigerator, 9/16-17 *(with pictures)*
refugee camp, 12/180
rehearsal, 3/152-153
reindeer, 12/50 *(with picture),* 13/43 *(with picture)*
religion
  buildings and, 13/122-125 *(with pictures)*
  food and, 12/57
  see also specific religions
religious dance, 3/178
Remembrance Day, 14/166-167 *(with pictures)*
remote control, 9/84 *(picture),* 9/92-93 *(with pictures),* 9/109 *(picture)*
reproduction, 5/10
  human, 11/59, 11/92-93 *(with pictures)*
reproduction, plant
  without seeds, 5/32-33 *(with pictures)*
  with seeds, 5/20-29 *(with pictures)*

s

181

T

t (letter), rhyme about, 1/61
tabla (musical instrument), 3/125
    (with picture)
Table Manners (Burgess), 1/88
tadpole, 4/86-87 (with pictures)
tag game, 12/84-85 (with pictures)
tail, of amphibian, 4/88-89 (with
    pictures)
Taj Mahal (India), 13/13 (picture),
    13/162 (picture)
talent, 11/130-131 (with pictures)
Tale of Peter Rabbit, The (Potter),
    3/73 (with pictures)
talking, see speaking
tally marks, 10/133 (with picture),
    10/147
tamandua, 4/21 (picture)
Tamil (language), 12/131 (picture)
Tamil (people), 12/26 (with picture)
tandem bicycle, 9/42 (picture)
Tanganyika, Lake (Africa), 13/14-
    15
tangram (pattern), 10/32-35 (with
    pictures)
tanka (art), 3/26
tanker, 9/69 (with picture)
Tanzania (Africa), 12/40 (picture)
    drum messages in, 12/147 (with
    picture)
tap dance, 3/180-181 (with picture)
tape recorder, 9/28-29 (with
    pictures)
tarantula, 4/137 (with picture)
tartan (material), 12/29 (picture)
Tasmania, 13/25
taste (sense), 11/63, 11/68-69 (with
    picture), 11/82-85 (with pictures)
    test of, 11/84 (with pictures)
taste buds, 11/82-83 (with pictures)
Taylor, Jane (poet)
    Star, The, 1/44
tea, 12/39 (picture)
    oolong, 12/69
teacher, 12/113 (picture), 12/124
    (with pictures), 13/79 (picture)
    of learning-disabled child, 15/110-
    111
    of physically-disabled child, 15/116
    of school-age child, 15/65, 15/71-
    73 (with pictures)

school problems and, 15/79,
    15/81
see also **education; school**
Teacher's Day (holiday), 14/144
    (with picture)
team, 12/172-175 (with pictures)
tear gland, 11/106 (with picture)
tears, 11/70
technician, 9/147, 9/168 (picture)
technology
    dangers of, 9/178-179 (with
    picture)
    helping people, 9/176-177 (with
    pictures)
    see also **invention**
tectonic plate, 6/48-49 (with
    pictures)
teeth, human
    baby, 11/14
    caring for, 11/172-175 (with
    pictures), 15/59 (with picture)
    eating and, 11/53
    of school-age child, 15/69
    permanent, 11/14-15 (with
    pictures)
teeth, of crocodile, 4/80 (picture)
teeth, on gear, 8/24 (with picture)
telephone, 9/8 (picture), 9/11
    (picture), 9/100-101 (with
    pictures), 9/149 (picture), 12/151
    (with picture), 13/29 (picture)
    fiber-optic system, 8/136-137 (with
    picture)
    microprocessor in, 9/34 (with
    picture)
    pay, 9/108 (picture)
    signal line for, 9/98-99 (with
    picture)
    tin-can (project), 8/146-147 (with
    picture)
    see also **cellular telephone**
telescope, 7/36, 7/44, 9/10
    (picture)
    Hale, 7/157 (picture)
    invention of, 7/144-145 (with
    picture)
    observatory, 7/150-151 (with
    pictures)
    of Herschel, 7/85, 7/156 (with
    picture)
    of Newton, 7/156 (with picture)
    reflecting, 7/101 (picture), 7/147
    (with picture)
    refracting, 7/146 (with picture)
    space, 7/183 (with picture)
    tabletop, 7/148-149 (with picture)
teletext, 12/150-151

television, 9/10 (picture), 9/35
    (picture), 9/88-89 (with pictures),
    12/150, 13/28 (with picture)
    child's viewing of, 15/53-54 (with
    picture), 15/60, 15/66, 15/94-
    95
    remote control, 9/92-93 (with
    picture)
tempera paint, 3/42-43
temperate forest community,
    5/56-59 (with pictures)
temperature
    lowest, 8/91
    measurement of, 9/14-15 (with
    pictures), 10/176-177 (with
    pictures)
    on Earth, 6/16-17 (with pictures),
    6/70, 6/168-169 (with picture)
    on Mercury, 7/66
    on sun, 7/10, 7/13, 8/115
    on Venus, 7/71
    see also **cold; heat**
temple, 13/122, 13/125
ten, in counting, see **number
    system**
Ten Commandments, 14/102-
    103
tendon, 11/45 (with pictures)
tennis, energy used in, 8/79 (with
    picture)
Tenochtitlan (ancient city),
    14/130
Tereshkova, Valentina
    (cosmonaut), 7/165 (with picture),
    7/173
tern, 4/153
terra-cotta sculpture, 3/80-83
    (with pictures)
terrain map, 13/129 (with picture)
terrarium, 5/128 (with picture)
tesserae (shapes), 10/40 (with
    pictures)
testicle, 11/59
tetromino (shape), 10/24 (with
    picture)
Thailand, 12/118 (picture), 12/137
    (picture), 14/75, 14/89 (with
    picture)
    family in, 12/10 (picture)
    food in, 12/48 (picture), 12/61
    (picture)
    garden in, 5/157 (picture)
Thanksgiving Day, 14/168-169
    (with pictures)
Thank Someone (Durkee), 12/42-
    43 (with pictures)
thatching, 12/126

183

U

u (letter), rhyme about, 1/61

Uganda, 13/39 *(picture)*

Ukraine, 3/130, 14/79 *(pictures)*

ultraviolet rays, 7/36, 7/183, 8/133 *(with picture)*

Uluru (Australia), 13/24-25, 162 *(picture)*

umbilical cord, 11/95 *(with picture)*, 11/96

umbrella, 9/149 *(picture)*

UN, see **United Nations**

uncle, 11/109, 11/111 *(with picture)*, 12/10, 15/62

underachiever, 15/80

UNICEF, 14/156, 15/117

unicycle, 9/51 *(with picture)*

Union of Soviet Socialist Republics, see **Soviet Union**

uniqueness
of human face, 11/11
of people, 11/130-131

United Kingdom, 12/41 *(picture)*, 12/169, 13/92, 13/99, 14/45, 14/166
cricket in, 12/91 *(with picture)*
etiquette in, 12/160-161 *(with picture)*
food in, 12/53, 12/68 *(with picture)*, 12/69
independence from, 14/32, 14/44, 14/114, 14/116, 14/151

school in, 12/121 *(picture)*
see also **England; Scotland; Wales**

United Nations, 12/182-183 *(with pictures)*
on rights of children, 15/117-119
see also **UNICEF**

United Nations Day, 14/156-157 *(with pictures)*

United States, 13/16, 14/115, 14/183
clothing in, 12/31 *(picture)*
eating customs in, 12/66-67 *(with picture)*
family in, 12/11 *(picture)*, 12/20 *(picture)*
food in, 12/56, 12/68 *(with picture)*
games in, 12/89, 12/91 *(with picture)*
kites in, 12/105 *(picture)*
language in, 12/128-129, 12/132
leader of, 12/178
learning in, 12/115, 12/126 *(with picture)*
measurement in, 10/163
special days in
April Fool's Day, 14/74
Christmas, 14/180
Columbus Day, 14/152
Father's Day, 14/105
Flag Day, 14/107
Halloween, 14/156 *(with picture)*
Independence Day, 14/116 *(with picture)*

Kwanzaa, 14/182 *(with picture)*
Martin Luther King, Jr., Day, 14/36-37 *(with pictures)*
Mother's Day, 14/94
Remembrance Day, 14/166-167
Thanksgiving, 14/168-169 *(with pictures)*
Valentine's Day, 14/45
toys in, 12/99 *(with picture)*, 12/101 *(picture)*
traditions in, 12/24-26 *(with picture)*
vacations in, 12/97

Unity, U.S. (spacecraft), 7/169 *(picture)*, 7/178 *(picture)*, 7/180 *(picture)*

universe
galaxies in, 7/130-131
number of stars in, 7/101
studying, 7/138-183 *(with pictures)*
see also specific topics, such as **planet**

uranium, 6/27 *(with picture)*

Uranus (planet), 7/61 *(picture)*, 7/64 *(picture)*, 7/84-85 *(with picture)*, 7/86, 7/90 *(with picture)*

urethra, 11/57 *(with picture)*

urine, 11/56

Ursa Major (constellation), 7/98-99 *(picture)*, 7/112 *(picture)*

uterus, 11/59

Utrillo, Maurice (artist), 3/59 *(with picture)*

V

v (letter), rhyme about, 1/62
vacation, 12/96-97 (with pictures),
    13/160-175 (with pictures)
  activities during, 13/168-169,
    15/98-99
  packing for, 13/166-167 (with
    pictures)
  planning, 13/136 (with picture),
    13/164-165 (with pictures)
  remembering events during,
    13/174-175 (with picture)
  see also **travel**
vacuum, 9/23
vacuum cleaner, 9/22-23 (with
    picture), 9/148 (picture)
vagina, 11/59, 11/96
Valencia (Spain), 14/66 (with
    picture)
Valentine, St. (Christian saint),
    14/45 (with picture)
Valentine's Day, 14/45-47 (with
    pictures)
valley, 6/60-61 (with pictures)
  in ocean, 6/68 (with picture)
Vancouver (British Columbia),
    14/114 (picture)
vanilla, 5/104
vanity, story about
  Emperor's New Clothes, The, 2/36-
    47
Vatican City, 13/23
Vega (star), 7/116, 14/126-127
vegetable, 11/159-163 (with
    pictures), 12/52-53 (with pictures),
    12/61
vegetarian, 12/57
vein, 11/47 (with picture)
vein, in rock, 6/34 (with picture)
Venezuela, 14/121
  nursery rhyme from
    Lullaby to a Naughty Baby, 1/49
Venn diagram, 10/74-75 (with
    pictures)
vent
  house, 9/154 (picture)
  submarine, 9/70 (with picture)
Venus (goddess), 7/91 (with picture)

Venus (planet), 7/64 (with picture),
    7/70-71 (with pictures), 7/91 (with
    picture), 7/145 (with picture)
Venus's-flytrap, 5/49 (with picture)
Vermont, 12/58 (picture)
Versailles, Palace of (France),
    13/92-93 (with picture)
vertebrate, 4/108
Very Clumsy Click Beetle, The
    (Carle), 3/19 (with picture)
Very Hungry Caterpillar, The
    (Carle), 3/18 (with picture)
Veterans Day, 14/166-167
veterinarian, 4/182 (with picture)
vibration, sound, 8/140 (with
    picture), 8/144, 8/147, 9/30-31,
    9/86, 11/76
  in musical instrument, 3/115-122,
    3/120-121
  in telephone diaphragm, 9/100-101
  loudness and, 8/157
  of vocal cords, 3/113
  pitch and, 8/148-149
Victoria (queen of Britain), 14/92
    (with picture)
Victoria, Lake (Africa), 6/97
Victoria Day, 14/92 (with picture)
Victoria Falls (Africa), 13/15,
    13/118 (with picture)
vicuña, 5/84
videocassette recorder, 9/35
    (picture)
video game, 8/179 (with pictures)
video screen, 8/179
videotape, 9/29 (with picture)
Vietnam, 12/48, 14/42
viewfinder, of camera, 8/127
    (with picture)
Viking 1 (spacecraft), 7/77
Viking 2 (spacecraft), 7/77
Vikings (people), 3/10 (with picture)
village family, 12/13 (with picture)
Villa Savoye (Poissy, France),
    13/115
vine, 5/75 (with picture)
vinegar, 8/55
Vinson Massif (mountain,
    Antarctica), 13/21
vinyl, 9/141 (with picture)
violence, on television, 15/53,
    15/66, 15/94

violet (color), 8/131, 8/133
violin, 3/116 (with picture)
viper, 4/75
virtues, poems about
  Enjoy the Earth, 1/84
  Good, Better, Best, 1/89
  One Thing at a Time, 1/89
  Patience, 1/89
  Say Well and Do Well, 1/89
  Table Manners, 1/88
  Thingumajigs, 1/90-91
  Whatever You Do, 1/89
virus, 11/146-147
Vishnu (god), 13/125, 14/63 (with
    picture)
vision, see **sight**
vitamin, 11/159, 11/160, 11/169
vocal cords, 3/112-113 (with
    picture), 11/74-75 (with pictures)
voice, 11/74-75
  see also **speaking**
voice box, see **larynx**
volcano, 6/18, 6/53-55 (with
    pictures), 6/101 (with picture),
    7/86
  climate change and, 6/156-157
    (with picture)
  Giant's Causeway, 6/28-29
  in ocean, 6/68 (with picture)
  island, 6/56-57 (with pictures), 6/69
    (with picture)
  lake, 6/95 (picture)
  rock from, 6/23
Volga River (Europe), 13/23
volleyball (sport), 12/91 (picture)
volume (measurement), 10/159
    (with picture), 10/170-171 (with
    pictures)
von Braun, Wernher (engineer),
    7/158
vorticella (animal), 4/117 (with
    picture)
Voyager 1 (space probe), 7/81,
    7/83
Voyager 2 (space probe), 7/81,
    7/83, 7/85, 7/86
vulnerable animal, 4/179 (with
    pictures)
vulture, 4/165 (picture), 4/178
    (picture)

186

X

Y

y (letter), rhyme about, 1/63
Y.A. Gagarin Center, 7/173, 7/174
yak, 5/84, 12/51 (with picture)
Yangtze River (China), 13/13
Yap Islands, 14/157 (picture)
yard (measurement), 10/163
yawning, 11/121 (with picture)

year
on Earth, 6/13, 7/72, 14/14-19
on Jupiter, 7/80
on Mars, 7/74
on Mercury, 7/67, 7/143
on Neptune, 7/87
on Pluto, 7/88
on Saturn, 7/82
on Uranus, 7/84
on Venus, 7/71
yeast, 5/51 (with picture), 9/119, 12/47

yellow (color), 6/106-107, 8/128, 8/131
Yellow (McCord), 1/75
Yellow Bottle (Cragg), 3/100 (picture)
yew, 5/44 (with picture)
  Pacific, 5/170
Yom Kippur, 14/140-141 (with pictures)
Your Nose Is Running (Moss), 1/23
yo-yo, 12/100
Yuma Indians, 1/37
yurt (tent), 12/12 (picture)

Z

Illustration Acknowledgments

The Publishers of *Childcraft* gratefully acknowledge the courtesy of the following illustrators, photographers, agencies, and organizations for illustrations in this volume. When all the illustrations for a sequence of pages are from a single source, the inclusive page numbers are given. Credits should be read from top to bottom , left to right, on their respective pages. All illustrations are the exclusive property of the publishers of *Childcraft* unless names are marked with an asterisk (*).

Cover	Boys running through field—© Philip & Karen Smith, Tony Stone Images*; Boys on tire swing—© Lori Adamski-Peek, Tony Stone Images*; Tongan girl dancing—© Anna A. Zuckerman, Photo Edit*; African-American girl reading—© Cathy Melloan*	58-59	CHILDCRAFT photo
		62-63	© Grantpix, Monkmeyer*
		64-65	© Jon Feingersh, The Stock Market*; © Victoria Beller-Smith*
Back Cover	© Cathy Melloan*	66-67	© Don Smetzer, Tony Stone Images*
1	© Lori Adamski-Peek, Tony Stone Images*; © Anna A. Zuckerman, Photo Edit*; © Cathy Melloan*	68-69	© Lawrence Migdale*
		70-71	© Lawrence Migdale*
		72-73	CHILDCRAFT photo by Steve Hale; © David R. Frazier*
4-5	© Ariel Skelley, The Stock Market*; CHILDCRAFT photo by Steve Hale; CHILDCRAFT photo; © Lawrence Migdale*	74-75	CHILDCRAFT photo
		78-79	© Merrim, Monkmeyer*
		82-83	© Shackman, Monkmeyer*
6-7	© Lawrence Migdale*; © Victoria Beller-Smith*	84-85	© Jon Feingersh, The Stock Market*
8-9	CHILDCRAFT photo by Steven Spicer	90-91	CHILDCRAFT photo
10-11	CHILDCRAFT photo by Steven Spicer	94-95	© Cathy Melloan*
16-17	CHILDCRAFT photo by Steven Spicer	96-97	© Superstock*
34-35	CHILDCRAFT photo by Steven Spicer	98-99	© Jennie Woodcock, Corbis*
46-47	© Jon Feingersh, The Stock Market*	100-101	© Cathy Melloan*
48-49	© Jon Feingersh, The Stock Market*	102-103	© Armstrong, Zefa Picture Library*
50-51	© Eric Larravdieu, Tony Stone Images*; © Ariel Skelley, The Stock Market*	104-105	© David Young Wolff*
		108-109	© Mary Kate Denney, Tony Stone Images*
52-53	© Superstock*; © Grantpix, Monkmeyer*	112-113	© Cathy Melloan*
56-57	CHILDCRAFT photo	116-117	© Lawrence Migdale, Tony Stone Images*